THE BATTLE
OF BRITAIN

AMAZING AND EXTRAORDINARY FACTS

THE BATTLE OF BRITAIN

Joseph Piercy

RYDON
PUBLISHING

A Rydon Publishing Book
35 The Quadrant
Hassocks
West Sussex
BN6 8BP
www.rydonpublishing.co.uk
www.rydonpublishing.com

First published by Rydon Publishing in 2021

A CIP catalogue record for this book is available from the British Library.

ISBN: 978-1-910821-35-0

CONTENTS

INTRODUCTION

The Battle of Britain is the name given to a series of intense air battles between the RAF and the German Luftwaffe that raged in the skies over southern England through the summer and autumn of 1940. Conventional wisdom is that, although heavily outnumbered, the British forces, through sheer grit and determination, finally prevailed over the enemy and thereby secured a notable victory over their foe. The significance of the victory is often cited as the first chink in the hitherto air of Nazi military invincibility and the springboard from which Britain's war efforts progressed culminating in D-Day and Germany's eventual capitulation. But how much is this view actually accurate? How much is the product of propaganda and the often questionable fact that 'history is written by the victors?'

It was certainly a very close contest, to use a football analogy; (comparisons with the beautiful game and matches between England and Germany are the mainstay of tabloid jingoism in Britain), the 'battle' was a classic 'game of two halves'. The Luftwaffe were certainly much better prepared at the start of the battle. They had a very clear numerical advantage in terms of firepower but perhaps more importantly their pilots had far more aerial combat experience having been extensively used during the invasions of Poland and The Battle of France.

Britain meanwhile had suffered considerable losses in the attempted defence of France. After the time of the evacuation of Dunkirk from May to June 1940, the RAF had been reduced to only 36 Squadrons in active service with an operational strength of 331 single-engine fighters (the fabled Spitfires and Hurricanes). Air Chief Marshal Sir Hugh Dowding

(1882–1970) had advised Sir Winston Churchill of the need to preserve Britain's air defences in the face of probable Luftwaffe bombing raids until suitable replacements and reinforcements could be produced for the hundreds of lost aircraft. The RAF certainly started the battle very much on the back-foot and there were serious concerns at how long a prolonged aerial war of attrition could be sustained for.

One area of historical contention surrounds the extent to which Hitler actually intended to invade Britain as outlined in the plans for Operation Sea Lion. There is some historical evidence to suggest that, at least initially, Hitler favoured a negotiated peace treaty, concerned perhaps at the possibility of the USA entering the war. In any event, after his overtures to Churchill were firmly rebuffed, Hitler's plan to attempt to cripple Britain's air defences ahead of a possible invasion began to progress.

Despite some early successes for the Luftwaffe, as the summer wore on, the battle became a much more even-handed affair. Part of this was down to the different strategic approaches adopted by the Luftwaffe and Fighter Command respectively. Hugh Dowding favoured scrambling small numbers of fighters to meet the German bomber convoys and disrupt and disperse their formations. This had the effect of conserving RAF aircraft resources during the vital first few weeks of the battle while British aircraft production built up a head of steam. The Luftwaffe's tactic of sending tight, close formations of bombers with fighter escorts, thereby reducing the effectiveness of their main weapon, the Messerschmitt Bf 109, also had a part to play. Fighter Command also had the advantage of fighting over home soil enabling their planes to return to their bases to rearm and refuel before setting out again.

Britain, thanks to Hugh Dowding, had developed a sophisticated integrated air defence system of which the Luftwaffe were sceptical. German intelligence was aware of Britain's developments with radar technology but did not believe that the system was particularly effective. Many senior Luftwaffe commanders including Hermann Göring, took the view that radar was not necessarily disadvantageous as their key strategy was to lure as many RAF Fighter's in to the air as possible where, hypothetically, the superior numbers of Luftwaffe planes could shoot them down. One often stated argument is that Göring made an error of judgement by switching attention from the strategic bombing of airfields and Chain Home radar stations in favour of an all-out bombing offensive on London. The answer to this can only be speculated on and it is worth noting that if the planned invasion of September 1940 was to take place, Germany was rapidly running out of time to disable Britain's air defences.

So did the fabled 'Few' of the RAF actually 'win' The Battle of Britain? Luftwaffe 'Ace' Adolf Galland didn't think so, holding firm that at best it was 'a draw' and Germany merely changed emphasis, eventually switching attention to the invasion of the Soviet Union. One 'fact' that is not disputable though is the extraordinary bravery and resilience of Allied airmen in resisting three and a half months in the face of an almost relentless and ferocious onslaught. There are many stories and tributes to individual acts of courage and valour explored in this book of amazing and extraordinary facts about The Battle of Britain. Ultimately the debate over the extent to which the RAF 'won' the battle needs to be measured against the catastrophic consequences if they had 'lost' it. The significance of the 'victory' in this respect was summed up by Winston Churchill in a famous speech to The House of Commons on 20 August 1940: 'Never in the field of human conflict was so much owed by so many to so few'.

Joseph Piercy
Brighton, 2021

Part One:
Preparations for Battle

The RAF, while performing admirably in The Battle of France, were nonetheless in disarray following the evacuation of Dunkirk. By 5 June 1940 it is estimated Fighter Command had only 330 operational single engine fighters. Britain had developed an air defence system but this hadn't been tested in full conflict conditions. This section looks at the preparations for the Battle on both sides.

WHO NAMED THE 'BATTLE OF BRITAIN'?
Churchill's 'finest hour' speech

On 18 June 1940, British Prime Minister Winston Churchill gave a speech to The House of Commons which contained the first recorded reference to 'The Battle of Britain'. Churchill had been Prime Minister for little over a month and was determined to cement the support of an all party coalition to unite behind the war effort. The evacuation of Dunkirk had led to calls for appeasement with Hitler, a course of action Churchill firmly rejected

Winston Churchill

out of hand. Churchill's main intention was to provide a report to the House on the condition of Britain's military resources and to convince any appeasers or waverers that it was vital to fight on despite the substantial losses the allies had suffered in France and across Northern Europe: 'What General Weygand has called the Battle of France is over... The Battle of Britain is about to begin'.

Following the reports from the military, Churchill moved on to delivering a powerful message about the moral duty Britain had to protect not only their national interests but also the freedom of smaller nations and allies and (with typical bombast) 'the survival of Christian civilisation'. Churchill finished his speech with the famous prediction: '...if the British Empire and its Commonwealth last for a thousand years, men will still say 'this was their finest hour'.'

DID YOU KNOW?

Churchill took great care when drafting his speeches, often adding revisions and corrections at the last minute or during the speech itself. The typescript of 'their finest hour' speech shows the final sections to be laid out in blank verse, this was possibly deliberate to give the impression of the speech being a powerful psalm or sermon.

OPERATION SEA LION
Hitler's Plan to Invade Britain

On the 16 July 1940 Adolf Hitler issued Führer Directive Number 16 (subtitled 'On preparations for a landing operation against England'). Hitler had become impatient with the refusal of the British government to negotiate a peace treaty, which he and his generals thought likely following the evacuation of Dunkirk. In the directive Hitler writes: 'Since England, in spite of her hopeless military situation, shows no signs of being ready to come to an understanding, I have decided to prepare a landing operation against England and, if necessary, to carry it out. The aim of this operation will be to eliminate the English homeland as a base for the prosecution of the war against Germany and, if necessary, to occupy it completely'.

Plans were in place for a military invasion of the Soviet Union in 1941 and Hitler felt that a quick resolution of the

DID YOU KNOW?

Hitler's initial plans for Operation Sea Lion proposed invading the Isle of Wight and Cornwall first to establish military footholds before launching a full scale invasion force along the South East Coast from Ramsgate to Lyme Regis in Dorset. These ambitious plans were quickly revised in favour of a surprise attack at four landing spots in Kent and Sussex: Ramsgate, Folkestone, Bexhill and Brighton.

DID YOU KNOW?

Hitler made extensive plans for how a post invasion Britain should be governed if Operation Sea Lion had been a success. One of these was the forced deportation of all able-bodied men aged between 17 and 45 to the Reich to work as slave labour in mines and industrial complexes. One of the more bizarre plans was to dismantle Nelson's Column and move it to Berlin as Hitler admired Nelson as a military commander.

war with Britain would enable Germany to redirect military resources to the Eastern front. Hitler named the proposed operation Seelöwe (sea lion) and instructed his generals to engage in the preparations immediately, demanding that all necessary planning be in place by the middle of August 1940 with a view to a September invasion.

Luftwaffe Insignia

Several of Hitler's high ranking generals, including Commander In Chief of the *Luftwaffe* Herman Göring, were opposed to Hitler's plans. One cause for concern was the perceived superiority of the Royal Navy over the *Kriegsmarine* (German Navy) which would present considerable difficulties for an invasion by sea.'

Hitler calculated that the threat from the Royal Navy would be considerably reduced without protection from the air. His plan was to neutralize Britain's air defences by strategically bombing airstrips, aircraft hangars, ports and industrial complexes. Once aerial superiority had been established, Britain would either be forced in to a compromise treaty/armistice or face a full-scale invasion. The Luftwaffe had considerable fire-power at their disposal and the Germans clearly believed that the numerical advantage in terms of the number of aircraft and pilots would enable them to over-power the RAF.

EXTRAORDINARY FACT

Although The Battle of Britain is of considerable significance with regard to the history of The Second World War, there is no firm consensus on the dates of when it started and when it ended. The Luftwaffe began making small scale night raids and sorties over Britain in mid to late June 1940. The frequency of these raids rapidly increased with the first daylight attacks taking place from early July. The main heat of the battle occurred between August and mid-September. Royal Airforce historians officially cite The Battle of Britain as taking place between 10 July and 31 October. This is disputed by German historians who place the battle as lasting from July 1940 to June 1941. The main reason for the discrepancies is that British historians distinguish between The Battle of Britain and The Blitz, the latter being the eight month long systematic bombing campaign of British cities and ports which began in mid-September 1940. German war historians argue that the Blitz was merely a change in strategy and a switch from day time dog fights to almost exclusively night bombing raids.

GERMANY'S SECRET AIR FORCE
The Lipetsk Fighter Pilot School

Under the conditions of The Treaty of Versailles, signed
on 28 June 1919, Germany was banned from operating
any form of air force, civilian or military. The treaty also
initially prohibited the production and import of any form
of aircraft in or out of Germany and forced Germany to
relinquish control of its airspace. By 1922 however, Germany
petitioned the Allies for the restrictions to be relaxed so that
aircraft could be used for mail deliveries and transportation
of goods to aid the redevelopment of the German economy.
In 1923 Germany regained control of their airspace and the
restrictions on the use of aircraft was partially lifted, allowing
Germany to produce planes for commercial and recreational
purposes. The restrictions on the operation and production of
aircraft for military purposes remained.

Although officially Germany was reluctant to break the
Treaty of Versailles, the crippling effect of the financial
sanctions and reparations the treaty placed upon the country
left the German economy virtually bankrupt. In 1923
Germany defaulted on reparation payments to France,
resulting in the French army occupying the Ruhr region.
The Ruhrkampf – as it is known, caused widespread unrest in
Germany and arguably further crippled the German economy
leading to hyperinflation and mass unemployment. The British
government were opposed to the French occupation of the
Ruhr and with the support of the US brokered a compromise
deal (The Dawes Plan) which lightened some of the pressure
on German reparation payments.

The *Ruhrkampf* had deeply hurt German pride and is

believed to have been the catalyst for the clandestine German rearmament programme. The German military, the *Reichswehr*, were mindful of the importance of air warfare and concerned not to fall too far behind other powers in terms of research and development.

EXTRAORDINARY FACT

The Treaty of Versailles imposed strict military sanctions and disarmament protocols on Germany. However, there is considerable evidence that the post-World War I German government indulged in various deception tactics to trick the Allied inspectors overseeing the decommissioning of German military hardware. Dutch aircraft designer and manufacturer Anthony Fokker, is believed to have assisted the German government in 'hiding' aircraft from the Allies. Fokker produced several successful aircraft for the German air force during World War I including the Fokker Dr.I, best known as the plane flown by Manfred von Richthofen, aka 'The Red Baron'. At the end of the war, Fokker and his company associates concealed and secreted aircraft in barns and buildings throughout the German countryside. Fokker, presumably in collusion with the German government, somehow managed to acquire an export licence. By surreptitiously putting airframes on trains under tarpaulin and packing disassembled parts into grain containers, Fokker began smuggling aircraft across the Dutch German border. It is estimated Fokker successfully smuggled 120 Fokker D.VII fighter planes, over four hundred engines and $8 million worth of parts and materials. Fokker's plunder was easily enough for him to set up a new aeroplane manufacturing business in Amsterdam.

The German Army ordered 100 new aircraft from Fokker in the Netherlands, among them 50 newly developed Fokker D.XIIIs. Additionally, the German Navy had also ordered a small number of planes. However, banned from training or even owning military aircraft, the *Reichswehr* were in a predicament as to what to do with the planes.

Since the signing of the Treaty of Rapallo in 1922 (effectively a mutual non-aggression pact), Germany had been building secret relations with the Soviet Union. In 1923 the German aircraft manufacturer Junkers opened a production facility for military aircraft just outside Moscow, supposedly to fulfil orders for the Soviet air force. Germany hatched a plan with the Soviets to set up a secret fighter pilot and research centre at Lipetsk in central Russia.

Fokker D.XIIIs in Lipetsk

DID YOU KNOW?

The accounts of the Dutch Aircraft Factory, the aircraft manufacturing company Anthony Fokker set up in Amsterdam, have no record of the secret order for fighter planes to be sold to Germany. The accounts for 1923 do however cite an identical order supposedly from the Argentine government. Suffice to say, there are no records of Argentina buying war planes from Holland in the 1920s.

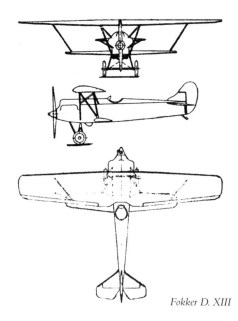

Fokker D. XIII

The Lipetsk Fighter Pilot School took two years to develop but had state of the art facilities. It is estimated that between 1926 and 1933, over two hundred German fighter pilots were trained in secret at Lipetsk, alongside hundreds of engineers and ground personnel. The official title for the facility was *Wissenschaftliche Versuchs-und Prüfanstalt für Luftfahrzeuge* (Scientific Research and Test Institute for Aircraft) – thereby disguising it as a scientific institution. The operation at Lipetsk closed by mutual agreement between the Soviet Union and Germany in 1933. At that point restrictions on the German military had relaxed and the divergent political directions of the two countries had started to cause friction. The legacy of Lipetsk was that it provided Germany with highly trained air military personnel who went on to form the basis for the Luftwaffe which was formed in 1935.

THE FOUR GROUPS OF 'THE FEW'
The Organization of RAF Fighter Command

RAF Fighter Command was established in 1936, replacing the previous organizational structure named The Air Defence of Great Britain. The previous organizational structure established in 1925 (ADGB) involved different elements of Britain's armed forces such as the Army and Royal Engineers working in conjunction with the RAF.

In 1936 however, the ADGB was abolished and sole responsibility for Britain's air defences was transferred to the RAF and divided into Fighter Command and Bomber Command. A key aspect of the fabled Dowding System (see page 24) was its unique organizational structure and chain

EXTRAORDINARY FACT

T.E. Lawrence, AKA 'Lawrence of Arabia', underwent basic training at RAF Uxbridge in 1922. Lawrence, a full colonel in the British army and something of a celebrity due to his heroics during the Arab Revolt in World War I, had become bored working as a diplomat at the Colonial Office under Winston Churchill and craved new adventures.

T. E. Lawrence

In order to hide his identity, Lawrence enlisted under the name of John Hume Ross. At his initial recruitment assessment, Lawrence was interviewed by Captain W.E Johns, author of the *Biggles* novels. Johns smelt a rat, or quite possibly recognized Lawrence, as he initially turned down his application on the grounds that he suspected Ross was a false name. However, Lawrence returned a few days later with a mysterious memo from a high-ranking RAF commander demanding that Lawrence/Ross be admitted to the training programme.

Lawrence stayed at RAF Uxbridge for a year before his true identity was exposed and he was expelled from the RAF because of the deceit. Lawrence re-joined the Army as part of The Royal Tank Corps, cheekily enlisting under the name of T.E. Shaw but loathed it. After writing numerous letters of apology, the RAF relented and allowed Lawrence to re-enlist in 1925 where he served until the mid 1930s.

DID YOU KNOW?

Many of the airfields used during World War II and particularly The Battle of Britain no longer exist or lie derelict and dormant. Some airfields, particularly the Satellite Aerodromes, have been converted for other purposes. RAF Ford and RAF Eastchurch have been converted into prisons and RAF Westhampnett is now the site of the Goodwood Motor Racing circuit.

of command. RAF fighter command was divided into four 'groups' (code numbered 10,11,12 and 13) of squadrons geographically spread across Britain, each with responsibility to defend an identified and localized area. Each 'group' had a number of airstrips assigned to their squadrons which were subdivided into three types: Group Headquarters, Sector Stations and Satellite Aerodromes.

Group 11, for example, was assigned to defend London and the South East, and was by far the biggest of the groups and was involved in the fiercest combat action.

The Group Headquarters (GH) of Group 11 were housed at RAF Uxbridge on the outskirts of Greater London. The GH at Uxbridge was well disguised due to its location and appearance of being a country house estate. The site, formerly known as Hillingdon House, was purchased by the British Government during World War I and had served mainly as a training facility during the inter-war years.

RAF Uxbridge served a vital role during The Battle of Britain as its Operations Room, housed in an underground bunker, was responsible for disseminating information to seven

Sector Station (SS) airfields, including RAF Biggin Hill and RAF Tangmere which played key roles in the war. In addition to the Sector Stations, Group 11 also rotated squadrons around a further seventeen Satellite Aerodromes or temporary airfields.

Group 11 Battle of Britain Airfields

Group Headquarters – RAF Uxbridge

Sector Stations – RAF Biggin Hill, RAF Debden, RAF Hornchurch, RAF Kenley, RAF Northolt, RAF North Weald, RAF Tangmere

Satellite Aerodromes – RAF Croydon, RAF Detling, RAF Eastchurch, RAF Ford, RAF Gosport, RAF Gravesend, RAF Hawkinge, RAF Hendon, RAF Lee-On-Solent, RAF Lympne, RAF Manston, RAF Martlesham Heath, RAF Rochford, RAF Stapleford, RAF Tawney, RAF Thornley Island, RAF Westhampnett, RAF West Malling

---

THE MAJOR PLAYERS:
*Sir Hugh Dowding, Architect of Britain's Revolutionary
Air Defence System*

In 1934 the RAF undertook a series of war game exercises aimed to test Britain's air defences in the face of large scale bomber attacks on London and other major cities. The results of these exercises showed a considerable time delay in relating knowledge of an impending attack fast enough to scramble fighters to mount an effective defence.

When Hugh Dowding became Air Officer Commanding-in-Chief of Fighter Command on its creation in 1936, he set about resolving the problem. Dowding's plan was to form a strong hierarchy within Fighter Command, where information would pass down the chain of command and, in the process, would be filtered and directed to the most relevant recipients. The speedy dissemination of information was made possible by a special telephone network, the lines of which were protected by being buried underground. Dowding, in his previous role as Air Member for Supply and Research, had

Sir Hugh Dowding

approved funding for the development of radar and was keen to integrate the new technology.

At the top of this hierarchy was Fighter Command Headquarters at RAF Bentley Priory, Stanmore, Middlesex. Fighter Command maintained an overview of the whole battle situation right across the country. Information on enemy aircraft movements sent from radar stations and Observer Corps centres, along with information on the positions of friendly aircraft from RAF direction finding stations, was rapidly relayed to Fighter Command HQ.

RAF ground staff and Women's Auxillary Air Force (WAAF) 'plotters' then mapped out the progress and likely destinations of Luftwaffe raids using colour coded blocks which were moved around the large General Situation Map table by long magnetic rods. This enabled the Duty controller to then assign interceptor fighters from the relevant Group No. Squadrons by contacting the most appropriate Sector Stations Operations rooms.

The Sectors in turn, took responsibility for communicating information to pilots, selecting and scrambling the squadrons under their command in response to instructions from Group HQ and transmitting updated information via radio to airborne fighters.

To ensure a co-ordinated defensive response to air raids, Fighter Command also controlled the anti-aircraft guns and searchlights operated by the Army and the barrage balloons flown by RAF Balloon Command.

The 'Dowding System' proved to be very successful, largely due to the ingenuity and foresight of Hugh Dowding. By devising a system that was able to swiftly process and distribute the vast amount of information provided by radar and

Observer Corps centres, the system maximized the usefulness of that information, dramatically improving the effectiveness of Britain's air defences.

With access to accurate and timely information, the British fighters could operate very efficiently – flying out from their bases directly to their targets, engaging in combat and then returning home to refuel and re-arm ready for the next raid. Dowding favoured this tactic of short sharp interceptions from light squadrons in order to preserve the RAF's fighter plane resources. However, his tactics were at odds with other RAF commanders, most notably Trafford Leigh Mallory the commander of Group No. 12, who favoured Douglas Bader's 'Big Wing' strategy.

RADIO DETECTION FINDING (RDF)
A Key Part of British Air Defence

The role that radar stations played in the Dowding System cannot be over-estimated. Without the Chain Home stations, Fighter Command would not have been able to gain the vital time advantage needed to scramble their squadrons and anticipate the Luftwaffe bombers targets.

The Radio Detection Finding (RDF) system was the brain-child of radio-physicist Sir Robert Alexander Watson-Watt (13 April 1892–5 December 1973). Originally Watson-Watt worked for the Meteorological Office researching in to possible ways to track electrical storms via the radio signals produced by lightning. During the course of his experiments in the 1920s, Watson-Watt developed a High

Sir Robert Alexander Watson-Watt

Frequency Direction Finding system (known as Huff Duff) which was able to detect long distance radio signals. Huff Duff went on to play a key part in intercepting enemy radio signals and was particularly effective against U-Boats.

In 1935 Watson-Watt was invited by The Air Ministry to investigate newspaper reports that Germany was developing a 'death Ray' that could destroy aircraft via radio waves. Watson-Watt and his assistant Arnold Wilkins undertook a series of calculations and concluded that it wasn't actually possible. However, Wilkins reported back to the Air Ministry that the use of radio signals could be used to locate aircraft at long distances. A secret demonstration of the fledgling RDF system was carried out in February 1935 using short wave transmissions from the BBC's Daventry transmissions station which were successfully bounced off an aircraft circling a nearby airfield. Hugh Dowding was suitably impressed and immediately released funds for the development of Watson-Watt and Wilkins prototype device. Watson-Watt led the development of a practical version of this device, which entered service in 1938 under the code name Chain Home, leading to the building of Chain Home Stations along the south coast of England.

After the success of his invention, Watson-Watt was sent to the US in 1941 to advise on air defence after Japan's attack on Pearl Harbor. He returned and continued to lead radar development for the War Office and Ministry of Supply. He was elected a Fellow of the Royal Society in 1941, was given a knighthood in 1942 and was awarded the US Medal for Merit in 1946. Watson-Watt's system provided the vital advance information that helped the Royal Air Force win The Battle of Britain.

THE MAJOR PLAYERS:
Air Vice Marshall Sir Keith Park

Keith Park was born (1892–1975) in New Zealand and initially fought for the New Zealand Army in World War I. Park took part in the landings at Gallipoli and the attritional trench warfare that followed and received several commendations for his bravery. Following the evacuation of Gallipoli, Park enlisted in the British Army, joining The Royal Horse And Field Artillery (Park was a skilled equestrian) and was shipped to France where he took part in The Battle of The Somme. A classic case of 'out of the frying pan and in to the fire'. Towards the end of The Somme, Park was injured when a stray German shell blew him off his horse and he was dispatched to England to recuperate. His injuries were serious enough for Park to be declared 'unfit for action' and he was discharged from service.

Sir Keith Park

Undeterred by his injuries and experiences of war, Park enlisted in The Royal Flying Corps in January 1917, initially to train as a flight instructor. Park showed considerable skills as a pilot, despite only a few months of training, and by the summer of 1917 he returned to France joining 48 Squadron. Park rapidly rose through the ranks, scoring notable successes and downing or destroying over a dozen enemy fighters. After the armistice, Park remained in the RAF during the inter war years, holding a number of prominent posts and was instrumental in helping Sir Hugh Dowding in the creation and restructuring of Fighter Command in preparation for The Battle of Britain. As a reward for his service and loyalty, Dowding appointed Park Air Officer Commanding (AOC) No. 11 Group – the largest and most prestigious of the air defence groups.

No. 11 Group bore the brunt of the Luftwaffe raids during The Battle of Britain but Park displayed great tactical awareness and skill and was an extremely popular commander amongst the squadrons he controlled.

Unfortunately a long running feud with Air Vice Marshall Leigh Mallory (see The Big Wing Controversy) led to Park being relieved of his duties (he was replaced by Leigh-Mallory) as No. 11 Group AOC – a decision which Park remained

★ AMAZING FACT ★

During his tenure in command of No. 11 Group, Keith Park was required to travel regularly between sector stations and aerodromes. A highly skilled pilot, Park insisted on flying his personal Hawker Hurricane from RAF Uxbridge to the various airfields under his control rather than travelling by road. This inevitably put Park at considerable risk of skirmishes with the Luftwaffe en route to his destinations. Although such recklessness was frowned upon by some high-ranking members of Fighter Command – it enamoured Park to the pilots under his command who appreciated his willingness to join the fray and get his hands dirty if needed.

embittered about for the rest of his life.

Park continued to serve as an AOC for the rest of the war, first in Egypt and then the Mediterranean, where he played a key role in the defence of Malta. Ironically in 1944 he was made Air Officer Commander In Chief for the Middle-East, taking over from his old adversary Leigh Mallory who was killed in an air crash. After the war Park returned to his native New Zealand where he dabbled in local politics. He died in 1975 at the age of 82.

THE MAJOR PLAYERS:
Reichsmarschall Hermann Wilhelm Göring

Hermann Wilhelm Göring

Hermann Wilhelm Göring (1893–1946) was one of the most powerful figures in the Nazi Party (NSDAP), which ruled Germany between 1933 and 1945. Göring served in the Imperial German Army during World War I, first in the trenches as an infantry officer before transferring to the *Luftstreitkräfte* ('air combat forces') where he trained as fighter pilot. Göring quickly distinguished himself as a skilled pilot, gaining 'ace' status and by the end of the war claimed 22 aerial victories earning him the *Pour le Mérite* ('The Blue Max') medal. After the death of Manfred von Richthofen (aka 'The Red Baron') Göring was made commander of *Jagdgeschwader* 1 (Jasta 1) the

★ AMAZING FACT ★

Göring was an early member of the Nazi Party and close associate of Hitler who made him commander of the *Sturmabteilung* ('Storm detachment' or 'Stormtroopers'). During Hitler's failed *coup d'état* The Beer Hall Putsch in November 1923, Göring was shot in the groin but evaded capture and was smuggled by his wife to Innsbruck in the Austrian Alps. Göring received surgery on his wounds and recovered but developed an addiction to morphine which continued to plague him throughout his life.

'crack' German fighter wing known as 'The Flying Circus'.

When the Nazis seized power in 1933, Hitler appointed Göring Minister Without Portfolio and entrusted him the job of creating the Gestapo. Göring was instrumental in mobilizing the German economy for the preparations for war and the German rearmament program. Through his industrial contacts, Göring became one of the richest men in Germany and the second most powerful figure in the Nazi Party. Due to his background in aviation, Hitler appointed Göring Commander-in-Chief of the newly created Luftwaffe (air force), a position he

QUICK FACTS

• At the start of World War II, Göring gave a propaganda speech extolling the power and might of his Luftwaffe. In the speech Göring bragged 'if as much as a single enemy aircraft flies over German soil my name is Meier'. These words came back to haunt Göring when in May 1940 the RAF began bombing German cities. Hitler became increasingly impatient with the Luftwaffe's inability to adequately defend German cities from the raids as the war progressed and blamed Göring, whom he began to view as incompetent.

held until the final days of the regime. At the start of World War II in September 1939, Hitler designated Göring as his successor and deputy in all his offices. Göring distinguished himself during the Fall of France, in which the Luftwaffe played a key role, and was promoted to the specially created rank of *Reichsmarschall*, giving him seniority over all officers in Germany's armed forces.

In July 1940, Hitler began preparations for Operation Sea Lion, a proposed invasion of Britain. The role of the Luftwaffe was key to the chances of success. Although Göring was confident Britain's air defences could be overwhelmed, in private he had reservations about launching a full-scale invasion force by sea. The failure of the Luftwaffe to neutralize the RAF during The Battle of Britain was Göring's first

EXTRAORDINARY FACT

Hermann Göring was renowned for his extravagant and eccentric hobbies and tastes. He loved to throw lavish parties at Carinhall, his purpose-built hunting lodge. During the gatherings Göring would don various fancy dress costumes, such as medieval hunting attire, often changing his clothes several times during the parties. He also had a collection of expensive fur coats. Göring was fanatical about the arts, particularly opera, and amassed a large art collection housed in a private gallery at Carinhall. At his trial at Nuremberg, Göring was charged with the theft and plunder of the property and belongings of victims of the Holocaust – a fact that undermined his defence that he had no knowledge of the death camps and wasn't anti-Semitic.

notable military defeat. As the war progressed, Göring's standing with Hitler and by extension his influence within the Nazi regime began to wane. Göring found himself increasingly marginalized and devoted his time to acquiring property and, particularly, artworks, much of which was plundered from victims of the Holocaust.

Göring was informed by telegram that Hitler intended to remain in Berlin and commit suicide should the city fall in to Soviet hands. Göring sent a telegram to Hitler requesting his permission to take control of the Reich, a chain of command that Hitler had endorsed at the start of the war. The telegram was intercepted by Martin Boorman, Hitler's personal private secretary, who convinced Hitler that Göring was a traitor. Hitler subsequently issued a decree relieving Göring of his positions, expelling him from the Nazi party and ordering his arrest and execution on the grounds of high treason. Göring was captured by US troops at the end of the war and charged with conspiracy, crimes against peace, war crimes and crimes against humanity at the Nuremberg trials in 1946. During the trials Göring defended himself and repeatedly claimed that he had never been anti-Semitic and had no knowledge of the Nazi death camps. Göring was found guilty and sentenced to death by hanging. In response to the sentence, Göring requested that his execution be carried out by firing squad as befitting of a solder, stating that hangings were for common criminals and murderers. Göring's request was denied, although he escaped the indignity of the gallows by committing suicide by ingesting cyanide the night before the sentence was due to be carried out.

THE STARS OF THE SKIES
The Supermarine Spitfire

In 1931, an Air Ministry report called for the need to beef-up Britain's air defences with a new fighter plane capable of speeds of up to 250 mph. The job of designing such a machine was entrusted to R.J Mitchell (1895–1937), a prominent aeronautical engineer who designed racing sea planes, most notably the Supermarine S.6B which broke the world air speed record in 1931.

Mitchell's initial design was a single seater open cock-pit monoplane named Supermarine Type 224, a revolutionary design powered by Rolls Royce Goshawk engines with an innovative evaporative cooling system. The Air Ministry rejected Mitchell's design in favour of a more traditional biplane fighter the Gloster Gladiator. Mitchell was

The Supermarine Spitfire was the only British warplane to be in production throughout the entirety of World War II. The Spitfire entered mass production in 1938 with the last Spitfire built in Britain in 1948. In total 20,351 planes were produced at an average cost of £12,500 each (approximately £750,000 in modern money terms). In comparison to modern war planes however, the Spitfire seems unbelievably cheap with the F35 Fighter jet currently in production in Britain costing an estimated £125 million per plane.

QUICK FACTS

• Spitfires that had the capacity to carry bombs under their wings were modified to carry kegs of ale to drop on to the beaches of Normandy to provide sustenance for the first troops on 'The Longest Day'.

disappointed with being knocked back and along with his team of engineers at Supermarine, set about making a number of design modifications. Mitchell and his team reduced the wingspan by six feet and added other features such as a closed cockpit with oxygen breathing apparatus for flying at high altitude and a ground-breaking retractable undercarriage. Further revisions were made after – yet again – the design was rejected (such as thinner wings and adding new Rolls Royce Merlin engines) with the Air Ministry eventually commissioning the production of prototypes of the design in 1934.

The Supermarine Spitfire (known only as Prototype K5054 at the time) made its maiden flight on 5 March 1936 taking off from Eastleigh Aerodrome near Southampton. The eight minute flight was piloted by Captain Joseph Summers, the chief test pilot for Vickers. R.J Mitchell was in attendance to witness the maiden flight of his brainchild, although sadly didn't live to see the plane go in to full production as he died from cancer in 1937 aged 42.

Although the Air Ministry were impressed enough to

Spitfire

place an order for 300 Spitfires to be built by Supermarine in the summer of 1936, initial teething problems delayed delivery of the order. Supermarine were a relatively small company, albeit with highly skilled engineers, and had production lines for Walrus and Stranraer flying boats to juggle. In order to manage production schedules, Supermarine were forced to sub-contract the building of certain parts of the aeroplane to other companies. This outsourcing however caused further logistical delays and the first Spitfires only began rolling off the production line in the summer of 1938.

Supermarine Spitfire Specifications:

Type: Fighter / Interceptor – Fighter-Bomber
Crew: One
Length: 9.12 metres (29.9 ft)
Wingspan: 11 metres (36 ft)
Max Speed: 580 km/h (362 mph)*
Range: 637 km (395 miles)
Armaments: 8 Browning 303 machine guns
Engine: Rolls-Royce Merlin mkIII
*Maximum speed recorded by MK 11 Spitfire

THE UNSUNG STORY OF HAZEL HILL
How a 13-year-old schoolgirl helped to redesign the Spitfire

U ntil very recently, little was known of Captain Frederick Hill (1889−1959) and his daughter Hazel Hill (1920−2010) and the decisive contribution that they made to the development of the Supermarine Spitfire. Frederick Hill was born in to a working-class family in North London and showed considerable aptitude in science at school. Hill studied chemistry at The University of London and trained as a teacher before joining The Royal Navy Volunteer Reserve force after the outbreak of World War I. After receiving his commission, and in recognition of his considerable skills in science and engineering, Hill joined the newly formed Experimental Armaments Division ('EAD') of the Royal Naval Air Service. During his time with the EAD, Hill undertook pioneering research work into methods of mounting machine guns on seaplanes and developing gunsights for fighter pilots.

Frederick Hill

During the inter-war years, Hill was transferred to the newly formed RAF and continued his research and development work in to aircraft armaments. In 1931 Air Vice Marshall Hugh Dowding commissioned research projects in to the speed and accuracy of fighter plane armaments. Hill was put in charge of analysing all of the data from extensive air firing trials and producing reports and recommendations. Hill became convinced that the prototypes of new high speed fighter planes being developed at the time could be fitted with eight machine guns. The Air Ministry

DID YOU KNOW?

Hazel Hill struggled at school on account of her dyslexia and literacy issues but excelled at mathematics. After studying medicine at University, Hazel joined The Royal Army Medical Corps working as a junior doctor treating wounded and traumatised soldiers. After the war, Hazel became a GP in the recently established NHS and devoted herself to child health issues and published ground-breaking research into conditions such as anorexia and autism.

at that time believed that adding extra armaments would slow the planes down, so Hill enlisted the help of his 13-year-old daughter Hazel, a highly gifted mathematician, to work on the complex calculations, algorithms and graphs needed to prove his theory to the Air Ministry. Frederick and Hazel would spend hours preparing and modifying their calculations, often working until late into the night. The Hills calculated that the new generation of fighter planes that the Air Ministry were developing, in order to operate effectively, would need to be equipped with eight guns capable of firing 1,000 shots a minute. Captain Hills presented the mathematical evidence to the RAF's Air Fighting Committee in July 1934 and was able to convince them not only were eight mounted machine guns possible, they were essential for the RAF to have cutting edge air defences. Hazel Hill played an integral role in assisting her father with his calculations due to her extraordinary aptitude for mathematics. In June 2020, Hazel's story was made the subject of a BBC Documentary, with the RAF honouring the importance of her role in developing the iconic fighter jets used in The Battle of Britain.

THE SHADOW FACTORY PLAN
The Castle Bromwich Aircraft Factory

British shadow factories were the outcome of the Shadow Scheme, a plan devised in 1935 and developed by the British Government in the build up to World War II to try to meet the urgent need for more aircraft using technology transferred from the motor industry to implement additional manufacturing capacity. The Shadow Scheme was put under the control of Herbert Austin (1886–1941), the founder of Austin Motor Company, who was charged with the task of building nine new bespoke aeronautical factories and making the necessary modifications and extensions to existing facilities to accommodate aircraft production.

After the delays in the production of Spitfire orders in 1938, Austin approached Lord Nuffield (1877–1963), founder of

Castle Bromwich Aircraft Factory

Morris Motors Ltd, to oversee the building of a modern aircraft factory next to the Castle Bromwich Aerodrome near Birmingham. Such was the need to radically speed up production, modern precision machine tools were installed while the factory buildings

QUICK FACTS

• Of the 20,351 Spitfires ever built only 238 survive in the world today. Many of the planes are exhibits on display in museums and other facilities across the globe. Of the 110 Spitfires in the UK, around 50 are still airworthy and are a popular attraction at air shows and anniversary celebrations.

were still under construction. The Air Ministry had placed an order for 1,000 Spitfires but initially the largely local workforce struggled to transfer their motor manufacturing skills to the precision engineering required for aircraft production.

Despite Lord Nuffield's pledge that his new factory would have the capacity to produce 60 aircraft a week, by May 1940, not a single Spitfire had been built. Lord Beaverbrook (1879–1964) the newly appointed Minister for Aircraft Production, took personal control of the project. Beaverbrook sacked Lord Nuffield and handed management of the factory over to Vickers-Armstrong engineering company. The new management immediately drafted in highly skilled engineers from Supermarine and production gradually improved. During The Battle of Britain, Castle Bromwich produced a hundred Spitfires between June and September 1940, providing the RAF with vital back-up firepower. Throughout World War II, Spitfire production at the plant rose dramatically and by the time the conflict ended in 1945, Castle Bromwich had produced 12,000 fighter planes, over half the total number of Spitfires ever built.

The foresight of the Shadow Factory scheme was born

out when the two original Spitfire factories at Woolston and Itchen, near Southampton, were destroyed during a Luftwaffe bombing raid on 26 September 1940, resulting in the deaths of 92 aircraft engineers and factory workers. The Luftwaffe had targeted the factories the previous month on 20 August but missed both targets. Following the narrow escape, much of the vital machinery had been relocated to smaller factories and other locations around the south east.

EXTRAORDINARY FACT

9,000 Miles of Concrete...

Following the failure of the Munich Agreement in 1940 and with war seemingly inevitable, Britain began a rapid expansion of its air fields. This work was undertaken by the Air Ministry Directorate General of Works and it is estimated that between 1939 and 1944 the AMDGW spent over £600 million on building, renovating and repairing airfields. This amounted to the total area of concrete laid for runways, perimeter tracks and aircraft dispersal points of 160 million square yards. Sir Archibald Sinclair, the Secretary of State for Air reported to Parliament that this amounted to a 14,484 km (9,000-mile) long, 9.14 m (30 feet) wide road between London and Beijing. To produce and transport such a mind-boggling amount of concrete would require a huge convoy of lorries stretching one and a half times around the world at the Equator.

BURIED TREASURE?
The Hunt for Lost Spitfires in Burma

In 2012, British farmer, David Cundall, sparked a media frenzy across the world by claiming the existence of a Spitfire burial ground in Myanmar (formerly Burma). According to Cundall, he was told twenty years previously by a veteran of the Burma campaign in World War II of a cache of up to 140 Spitfires that had been shipped to an airstrip in Burma formerly known as RAF Mingaladon.

The story alleges that at the end of the war in the Pacific, the RAF had dismantled the planes and packed them in to crates to be returned to the UK. However, logistical problems ensued and so rather than allowing the planes to fall in to the hands of the Japanese, the RAF buried them under the airfield for safe keeping. Initially the Myanmar authorities allowed for some minor excavations at the site but quickly withdrew permission for more detailed exploration as the former RAF base is now Yangon International Airport, Myanmar's busiest airport hub.

• In terms of the numbers of pilots with combat experience, the RAF was very ill-prepared at the start of the war compared with the Luftwaffe. Some newly qualified pilots were thrown in to the heat of the battle having only ten hours of solo flying experience under their belt. During The Battle of Britain, a fighter pilot's life expectancy was 87 flying hours, which equates to four weeks in combat. The average age of an RAF pilot was just 22.

DID YOU KNOW?

The RAF were not the only air force to fly Spitfires during World War II. Ten different countries were either loaned or purchased the iconic fighter plane, including the US, Australia, Canada, France and The Soviet Union. When the first United States Army Airforce squadrons arrived in Europe when America entered the conflict in Europe in 1942, they were initially short of interceptors and fighters and so used Spitfires. The fighter was one of the only non-American built planes the US used in the conflict.

US pilots preparing to fly a Spitfire

Undeterred, Cundall returned a second time after receiving funding from a Belarussian internet company Wargaming. net and this time used satellite ground penetrating radar to attempt to locate the crates. The spoils would be considerable if the planes were to be found as working Spitfires are worth in the region of £3 million each. The media furore around the story sparked the interest of the Prime Minister at the time, David Cameron, who allegedly negotiated with the Myanmar authorities for guarantees the planes would be returned to the UK if discovered. However, up until this point, the only crate dug up contained some pieces of rusted barbed wire fencing.

QUICK FACTS

• On the first Spitfires, designer RJ Mitchell used a combination of flushed and rounded rivets. Testing showed that by using more expensive flushed rivets on aerodynamic surfaces, it could increase speed by 22mph. There are 80,000 rivets on a Spitfire.

Part Two: The Early Skirmishes

Following Germany's rapid territorial gains in
the Battle of France, the Luftwaffe had to reorganize
its forces, set up bases along the coast, and rebuild
after heavy losses. The small-scale bombing raids that
began The Battle of Britain were primarily training
exercises to try out new methods. Known in Luftwaffe
terminology as Störangriffe ('nuisance raids') the
raids involved small numbers of aeroplanes and were
mostly conducted at night. Nonetheless the raids
gave the British the chance to analyse German tactics
and for Fighter Command to test its defences and
pilots to gain much needed combat experience. The
biggest test was still to come...

THE KANALKAMPF
Attacks On British Shipping Convoys –
July / August 1940

The Battle of Britain started relatively quietly, certainly
with respect for what was to come. The Luftwaffe began
with exploratory night raids in late June 1940, primarily to
test the possible strength of Britain's air defences. Hitler's
initial plan was to clear areas of the English Channel of
shipping to form a blockade and therefore neutralize the
superior power of the Royal Navy over the *Kriegsmarine*
(German Navy) by denying them access to British ports. This
required aerial attacks by the Luftwaffe on freight convoys

DID YOU KNOW?

The Royal Air Force (RAF) only came into existence towards the end of World War I. Previously both the British Army and the Royal Navy had airborne divisions known as the Royal Flying Corps (RFC) and the Royal Naval Air Service. These two divisions were amalgamated by the War Ministry to form the world's first independent air defence force. The formation of the RAF was not well received by the Royal Navy or The British Army who were now in direct competition for funding and resources from the government with a third party. This resentment and competition festered for many years and threatened to boil over during the *Kanalkampf* with the Navy complaining that the RAF was providing less than adequate support for shipping. In truth, Hugh Dowding was convinced, quite rightly, that a full-scale assault by the Luftwaffe was likely and convened to manage RAF resources to mount an effective air defence.

transporting goods and supplies on a route that ran from the Thames estuary along the south coast to the Bristol Channel. The German codename for this offensive was Operation *Kanalkampf* (Channel War).

Around a dozen freight convoys travelled through the Channel on a daily basis and required protection from attack from the air. Fighter Command found themselves in

EXTRAORDINARY FACT

Similar to the British armed forces there were tensions also between the various divisions of the German military. *Reichsmarschall* Hermann Göring (who was highly sceptical of Operation Sea Lion from the outset) was opposed to the *Kanalkampf* as he believed that the Luftwaffe were not adequately prepared for naval warfare. Göring argued that the operation amounted to establishing and maintaining a blockade which would then need to be effectively policed by *Kriegsmarine* (German navy).

Control of British sea communications would require support from the air, a strategy, in Göring's view, the Luftwaffe had little combat experience or training in and would leave their planes vulnerable to naval anti-aircraft defences. Hitler announced that a blockade was to be put into effect against Britain from 18 July and required the co-operation of the Luftwaffe with the *Kriegsmarine*. Göring was resistant to providing the necessary support due to a long standing feud.

Göring despised the *Kriegsmarine* and in particular its Commander-in-Chief *Großadmiral* Erich Raeder. In Göring's eyes, both Raeder and the navy represented the bourgeois clique of German society the National Socialist revolution had pledged to eliminate. Cooperation would at best be an uneasy alliance and Göring resented having to compromise with Raeder's orders and demands. Throughout the war the *Reichsmarschall* regularly obstructed the navy's calls for assistance in the conflict against the Royal Navy and commercial British shipping interests.

A British convoy under attack by German dive bombers, 1940

a quandary as on one hand the possibilities of losing large
numbers of aircraft in a battle of attrition over control of
the waterways was very likely, on the other hand, to provide
limited protection would leave many ships as sitting ducks.
Hugh Dowding (1882–1970) Air Chief Marshall of Fighter
Command (see page 23) had pressed Churchill for the freight
convoys to find alternative routes along the east coast of
Britain and via Scotland. Churchill however was keen to test
Britain's air defences and possibly use shipping as bait to lure
the Luftwaffe into open battle and potentially weaken their air
power resources, particularly their bombers.

The *Kanalkampf* – in terms of sustained attacks on British
shipping lanes – lasted between 4 July and 11 August. In
terms of establishing a decisive advantage in the conflict,

neither side could legitimately claim victory. The RAF lost an estimated total of 115 fighter planes with 42 damaged, in contrast to the Luftwaffe, who lost an estimated 215 aircraft including over 100 bombers and dive bombers with over a hundred damaged. In terms of casualties, 75 RAF pilots were killed with a further 19 wounded, in relation to 201 Luftwaffe airmen killed with at least a further 250 missing in action. Although the Luftwaffe suffered the greater losses in terms of planes and personnel, Britain lost over 50 ships during the period, including four Royal Navy destroyers. The considerable losses of merchant shipping led to the suspension of cargo convoys in the English Channel for several weeks during August and September 1940. Although Hitler's *Kanalkampf* operation had been partially successful in terms of disrupting British shipping, it had failed to significantly weaken Fighter Command's defences.

THE STARS OF THE SKIES:
The Messerschmitt Bf 109

In 1933 *Reichsluftfahrtministerium* (Reich Aviation Ministry) set up a design competition for a contract to build a new, bespoke, high performance modern fighter/ interceptor plane that could be mass-produced as part of Germany's rapid rearmament programme. Several of the leading aviation manufacturers were invited to take part in the competition and submit prototypes including Focke-Wulf, Heinkel, Arado Flugzeugwerke and the recently created firm BFW. After a series of head-to-head test flights BFW were awarded the contract for their prototype fighter/interceptor Messerschmitt Bf 109.

Messerschmitt Bf 109

Designed by maverick aviation designer Willy Messerschmitt, the Bf 109 adopted a revolutionary approach by adopting the concept of placing the most powerful engine into the smallest and lightest air-frame. Messerschmitt's aim was to produce an aircraft that could be easily mass-produced and repaired whilst retaining high levels of speed and manoeuvrability. Messerschmitt was also keen to reduce the number of parts used in aircraft production and introduced many innovations in air frame design.

The Bf 109 first entered active service during the Spanish Civil war (July 17 1936 – April 1 1939) where it was flown by several notable German Aces, including Werner Mölders and Adolf Galland. The plane was constantly modified during World War II with additional features added and by the end of the war the Bf 109K series boasted a 2,000 horse-power

QUICK FACTS

• The prototype Bf 109 that won the Reich Aviation Ministry (RLM) trials was powered not by a German engine but by a British produced Rolls-Royce Kestrel VI engine. The RLM acquired four Kestrel engines from Rolls-Royce in exchange for a Heinkel He 70 mail plane that Rolls Royce could use to test the performance and development of new engine designs. Therefore Rolls-Royce unwittingly contributed to the development of the Luftwaffe's most potent fighter plane.

Daimler-Benz engine and was capable of a top speed of almost 400 mph. Although faster than any of the RAF planes and with a more reliable engine, particularly in dive manoeuvres, the Bf 109 couldn't turn as sharply as the Spitfire (and to a lesser extent the Hurricane). This gave the RAF planes a distinct advantage in dog-fight situations, although the additional speed of the Bf 109 could be argued to counter to some extent.

During The Battle of Britain, the Bf 109 initially exerted some notable superiority over the RAF planes. However this can be explained by experienced Luftwaffe pilots with combat experience taking on their relatively green and poorly trained RAF opponents. A change in tactics by the RAF, coupled with the Luftwaffe using Bf 109s as escorts for bombers (which reduced their effectiveness) can be said to explain the shift in momentum.

Messerschmitt Bf 109

EXTRAORDINARY FACT

On 4 July 1940, HMS *Foylebank*, a converted merchant ship modified for anti-aircraft duties, was entering Portland Harbour in Dorset when she was attacked by a Luftwaffe bombing raid. The speed and ferocity of the attack took the *Foylebank* crew by surprise as they had mistaken the approaching planes as Allied aircraft. In a frenzied assault on the *Foylebank* that lasted a little over ten minutes, a total of 22 bombs were dropped on the largely defenceless ship. One gunner was able to make it to his post, Jack Foreman Mantle (aged 23) and managed to shoot down two Luftwaffe Stuka dive bombers. Mantle was posthumously awarded the Victoria Cross for bravery, thereby becoming only the second recipient of the award for 'valour in the face of the enemy' on UK soil at the time. The *London Gazette* of 3 September 1940 reported:

'Leading Seaman Jack Mantle was in charge of the Starboard pom-pom when FOYLEBANK was attacked by enemy aircraft on the 4 of July, 1940. Early in the action his left leg was shattered by a bomb, but he stood fast at his gun and went on firing with hand-gear only; for the ship's electric power had failed. Almost at once he was wounded again in many places. Between his bursts of fire he had time to reflect on the grievous injuries of which he was soon to die; but his great courage bore him up till the end of the fight, when he fell by the gun he had so valiantly served.'

The Messerschmitt Bf 109 remains one of the iconic aircraft of World War II nonetheless. It was produced in vast numbers (around 33,000) and was responsible for shooting down more Allied aircraft than any other Luftwaffe fighter.

Messerschmitt Bf 109 Specifications

Crew: 1

Wingspan: 10 m (32.82 ft)

Length: 9 m (29.53 ft)

Max Speed: 620 km/h (385 mph)

Range: 600 km (373 miles)

Armament: One 30-mm MK 108 (or 20-mm MG 151) cannon firing through the propeller shaft; two 13-mm MG 131 machine guns in cowling; additional cannon could be carried in pods under the wing.

Engine: Daimler-Benz DB 605/1,200

THE STARS OF THE SKIES:
The Hawker Hurricane

The received wisdom is that the Supermarine Spitfire 'won' The Battle of Britain and certainly in the eyes of the general public, the Spitfire was the glamour plane and the bane of the Luftwaffe. However, there is a compelling argument that the role played by the less prestigious Hawker Hurricane was equally fundamental to British success. In terms of numbers alone, Fighter Command had twice as many Hurricane Squadrons (36) as Spitfire Squadrons. RAF records cite that the Hurricane was responsible for destroying 1,593 enemy aircraft, 477 more than the Spitfire and over

Hawker Hurricane

half the number of RAF victories in total. Fighter Command deployed a total of 1,715 Hurricanes during The Battle of Britain, far in excess of the total numbers of other British fighter planes combined.

The Hurricane was designed by Sydney Camm (1893–1966), Hawker's chief aeronautical engineer, with the first prototype taking its maiden test flight on 6 November 1935, five months prior to the first Spitfire flight. Originally the early Hurricanes had fabric wings and two fixed machine guns above the engines but Camm continued to modify his design right up to the outbreak of hostilities in 1939. When The Battle of Britain started, the majority of Hurricanes had high performance metal stressed wings, allowing the plane to climb faster and more effectively and were armed with eight machine guns capable of firing off 1,000 shots per minute.

Some of the key advantages that the Hurricane had over the Spitfire was that it was cheaper, faster and easier to manufacture due to its relatively simple design. Teething problems with the production of Spitfires, which required

EXTRAORDINARY FACT

In the 1990s a group of metal detectorists discovered the wreck of a Battle of Britain Hawker Hurricane in a bog in Kent. The plane is thought to have been shot down by the Luftwaffe over Canterbury in August 1940 and the pilot bailed out leaving the plane to crash in to the bog. After carefully excavating and extracting the remains, the detectorists discovered around 40 per cent of the aircraft had been preserved.

The remnants of the Hurricane were purchased in 2017 by Peter Kilpatrick, a neurosurgeon and military history enthusiast. Mr Kilpatrick set about the seemingly impossible task of restoring the Hurricane to its former glory. After two years of painstaking work in an aircraft hangar at Elmsett Airfield, under the supervision of Hawker Restorations Ltd and a cost of £2 million pounds, the restored Hurricane took to the skies for its maiden flight with Peter Kilpatrick at the controls. This Hurricane is one of only 14 Hurricanes still air-worthy in the world.

considerably more man-hours, meant that the Air Ministry put considerable emphasis on Hurricane production in the lead up to the war.

Although not as fast and manoeuvrable as the Spitfire, the Hurricane was a more robust aircraft capable of absorbing more damage and was easier and quicker to repair and service. The Hurricane could turn quicker than enemy Messerschmitt Bf 109s making it formidable in a dogfight, although the German fighter's superior speed, especially when deploying dive and zoom attacks, made it vulnerable if out-numbered. As a consequence, Hurricanes were deployed largely to attack German bombers such as the Dornier Do 17 and Heinkel He 111, where the British fighter could exploit a considerable speed and manoeuvrability advantage.

Dornier Do 17

Hawker Hurricane Specifications

Type: Fighter/ Interceptor

Crew: 1

Length: 9.83 m (32.25 ft)

Wingspan: 12.19 m (39.99 ft)

Max Speed: 521 km/h (324 mph)

Range: 716 km (445 miles)

Armaments: 8 Browning 7.7mm Machine Guns

Engine: Rolls-Royce Merlin XX V-12

PROTECTING CONVOY PEEWIT
The Ferocious Battles of 8 August 1940

On the 7 August a large convoy of twenty-four merchant ships carrying coal and other industrial supplies set sail from the Medway ports on the evening tide. The convoy, codenamed 'peewit' (CW9), was escorted by two Royal Navy destroyers and eight smaller vessels equipped with anti-aircraft guns. The convoy was detected by German radar near Calais and as it entered the straits of Dover, the following morning, it came under a sustained attack from German E-Boats and squadrons of Stuka dive bombers. Although three of the smaller coaster merchant boats were sunk, 'peewit' managed to repel the attentions of the dive bombers and continue into the Channel.

SS Coquetdale

QUICK FACTS

• The SS *Coquetdale* was sunk by Luftwaffe Stuka dive bombers 15 miles off the coast of the Isle of Wight on 8 August 1940. Amazingly all of the crew survived. The wreck lies on the seabed in 40 m (130 feet) of water and is a popular spot for scuba divers.

As the convoy neared the Isle of Wight it was attacked a second time, this time by over a hundred Luftwaffe fighters and bombers. The Chain Home station at Ventnor was able to detect the ominous formation of German planes approaching the Solent and scrambled 18 Hawker Hurricanes and a Spitfire squadron to try to thwart the raid.

Ferocious air battles ensued with the RAF outnumbered by a ratio of three to one, and although the Allied pilots shot down seven enemy aircraft, they were unable to protect the convoy from further damage. As the remnants of the convoy 'peewit' limped towards the port of Swanage it was attacked for a third time, again by around 150 German aircraft. Two squadrons of Spitfires again attempted to engage the Luftwaffe in brutal dogfights and had some success in finally repelling them, thereby allowing the convoy to finally reach port.

Of the twenty-four ships that set sail from the Medway ports the previous day, only four arrived at Swanage unscathed, four had been sunk, with the rest badly damaged or forced to seek sanctuary in other ports. The RAF lost a total of 19 Hurricanes and Spitfires but claimed the shooting down of 31 German aircraft. Some historians cite the protection of the 'peewit' convoy as the date in which The Battle of Britain really began in earnest. It is certainly true that by the number of aircraft involved alone, the 8 August marked a dramatic escalation in hostilities.

Spitfire Squadron running to their planes

OPERATION EAGLE ATTACK
The Luftwaffe Changes Strategy

On 1 August 1940, *Reichsmarschall* Hermann Göring convened a conference of his Luftwaffe commanders at The Hague. Göring had received direct orders from Hitler to prepare for a sustained series of daytime assaults on RAF stations. At the meeting Göring is thought to have conceded that the *Kanalkampf* had failed to draw British fighter defences in to the air in large enough numbers for the Luftwaffe to effectively damage Britain's air defences. This was a deliberate tactic by Hugh Dowding and Keith Park, commander of Group 11, to preserve RAF resources. Only small waves of fighters were scrambled to protect shipping convoys and used on a relay basis, with planes returning to refuel and re-arm, whilst other small waves took to the air.

Göring had received inaccurate intelligence, and/or, had misinterpreted the RAF's small wave strategy as evidence that the RAF had scant resources in terms of planes available for battle. Göring informed his generals that he had calculated that the RAF had only 500 fighter planes and that a series of sustained heavy all-out attacks on airfields and radar stations in the south of England could virtually wipe out Britain's air defences within four weeks. This faulty intelligence was very much to the advantage of the RAF who in actuality had over 1,000 fighters at their disposal.

The operation was codenamed *Unternehmen Adlerangriff* ('Operation Eagle Attack') with the first day of the offensive *Adlertag* ('Eagle Day') initially scheduled for Saturday 10 August. In the event, poor weather caused the planned blitzkrieg to be suspended until 13 August.

EXTRAORDINARY FACT

On the morning of the *Adlertag* the weather was again very bad and Göring decided to further postpone the operation until later in the day. However, due to a breakdown in communications, several Luftwaffe units did not receive the postponement order. As a result several units took to the air at the scheduled time, among them bomber Unit KG-2 under the command of Johannes Fink. KG-2 had detailed 75 Dornier Do 17 bombers to attack and destroy RAF stations at Hornchurch and Eastchurch, on the Isle of Sheppey and were to be escorted by a squadron Messerschmitt Bf 110s.

The Luftwaffe planes set off towards their targets at 5am and met with their escort over the Channel. Messages to recall the planes were received by some of the Bf 110 pilots but they were unable to communicate with the bombers due to having the wrong crystals in their radios. As a result several of the escort fighters returned to base leaving the bombers unprotected. One German fighter pilot, Joachim Huth, tried to alert Fink by flying in front of Fink's Dornier Do 17 and performing acrobatic tricks, but Fink misinterpreted these actions as high spirits and continued on towards England. Although Fink and his fellow bombers attacked the airfield at Eastchurch they were intercepted on their return journey by No. 74 Squadron and without their escort lost five planes. KG-2 were actually lucky not to lose more aircraft under the circumstances and this was largely due to a miscalculation as to the bombers intended targets by radar plotters on the ground.

DID YOU KNOW?

Over claiming in aerial warfare is not uncommon, it was a key part of the propaganda war and a method of boosting moral amongst the respective air forces. During The Battle of Britain both sides claimed to have shot down and destroyed more enemy aircraft on the ground and in the air than they had in reality. RAF Fighter Command claimed 78 German aircraft shot down on 13 August 1940. Another source states that official RAF claims amounted to 64. Actual German losses amounted to 48 aircraft destroyed and 39 severely damaged. Conversely, the Luftwaffe claimed to have destroyed 70 Hawker Hurricanes and Spitfires in the air and a further 18 Blenheim bombers in the air alone. This was an exaggeration of about 300 per cent. Another 84 RAF fighters were claimed on the ground. Actual RAF losses in the air amounted to 13 fighters and 11 bombers, with 47 aircraft of various kinds on the ground.

Blenheim Bomber

ADLERTAG: 13 AUGUST 1940
'Eagle Day' Takes Off

After the 'false start' of the morning raids, Göring gave the order to recommence Adlertag at 2pm. Some 300 hundred Luftwaffe planes took to the air to undertake bombing raids predominantly on RAF airstrips, but also aircraft factories and the south coast ports of Southampton, Portsmouth and Portland in Dorset. In total the Luftwaffe attempted 485 bomber sorties and 1,000 fighter sorties in the afternoon and in to the night during Adlertag, with limited success.

Fighter squadron JG-53 were detailed to fly ahead of the bomber formations to provide a 'sweep' designed to

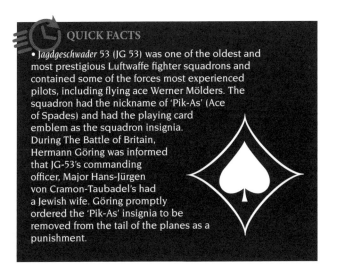

QUICK FACTS

• *Jagdgeschwader* 53 (JG 53) was one of the oldest and most prestigious Luftwaffe fighter squadrons and contained some of the forces most experienced pilots, including flying ace Werner Mölders. The squadron had the nickname of 'Pik-As' (Ace of Spades) and had the playing card emblem as the squadron insignia. During The Battle of Britain, Hermann Göring was informed that JG-53's commanding officer, Major Hans-Jürgen von Cramon-Taubadel's had a Jewish wife. Göring promptly ordered the 'Pik-As' insignia to be removed from the tail of the planes as a punishment.

Luftwaffe airmen of the Jagdgeschwader 53 (JG 53) fighter wing (also known as 'Ace of Spades') resting at an airfield in front of a Messerschmitt Bf 109 with an open cowling. Behind in the background is a Junkers Ju 52; KBK LW 3.

lure British fighter planes towards the west of England. This strategy however only succeeded in alerting Fighter Command to the impending assault and provided them with vital extra time to scramble their fighter defences. Thus by the time the German planes reached the coast of England 77 RAF fighter planes were in the air to meet them.

Attritional air battles ensued all along the South coast and continued in to the night. Many German bombers were forced to abandon their primary targets often ending up scattering their bombs over the countryside or rerouting to other targets of limited strategic relevance.

The ports of Southampton and Portsmouth were heavily attacked, as well as an airstrip at Andover. Although

Southampton suffered considerable damage, Luftwaffe intelligence had failed to identify a Spitfire factory on the docks and bombed a bicycle factory and furniture warehouse by mistake.

The raids continued under the cover of darkness with several major cities coming under attack but minimal damage was caused. The Castle Bromwich Spitfire factory was targeted and four bombs were dropped on the facility, but they failed to inflict enough damage to affect aircraft production.

The failure of *Adlertag* can be partly blamed on the low-level cloud and atmospheric conditions that made it difficult for the bombers to locate their targets. It was also an early example of the poor intelligence and serious navigational deficiencies which would plague the Luftwaffe throughout The Battle of Britain.

Part Three:
The Battle Intensifies

By 15 August 1940 The Battle of Britain was in full swing. This section looks at some of the key figures and personalities on both sides, the flying aces, the vital role of women and the outstanding contribution by dissident Polish airmen.

'BLACK THURSDAY':
15 AUGUST 1940
The Luftwaffe Attacks The North

On Thursday 15 August bad weather again delayed the Luftwaffe's planned raids. Göring summoned his commanders to a conference at Carinhall, his private hunting lodge in the Schorfheide forest. The meeting was ostensibly to review Operation Eagle Attack and discuss changes in strategy. Göring had been surprised by the scale of Britain's fighter defences and the effectiveness with which they had resisted the Luftwaffe assaults.

The decision was made to largely abandon the targeting of Home Chain Radar stations and concentrate instead on attacking Fighter Command airfields. There was a curious attitude amongst Göring and his commanders that the radar stations were hard to destroy as this required pinpoint accuracy from their bombers which were vulnerable to anti-aircraft defences. Actually, the Luftwaffe had caused more damage to Home Chain stations than they believed. In addition, several Luftwaffe commanders were not convinced that British radar systems were actually that effective and in any case, radar was not necessarily a bad thing as it lured British planes in to the air where the Luftwaffe thought they had a greater chance of destroying RAF planes.

Junker Ju 88 brought down

By the time the weather had cleared to plan the day's operations, Göring decided to involve Luftflotte 5, squadrons based at airfields in occupied Denmark and Norway and deploy them to attack RAF airfields in the north of England. Göring had calculated that the ferocity of Fighter Command's defences in the south could only have been achieved by leaving the north relatively defenceless. This assumption was based again on faulty German intelligence on the RAF's fighter resources. The Luftwaffe also took the curious decision to send the bombers of Luftflotte 5 to their targets with only a light protection escort (some Squadrons were completely unaccompanied). Alongside the inaccurate intelligence, a further reason to send the bombers unaccompanied was that the range of the Messerschmitt Bf 109s would not cover airfields in Scotland. Various airfields in North East England were attacked by 65 Heinkel He 111s escorted by 34 Messerschmitt Bf 110s, and RAF Driffield was attacked by 50 unescorted Junkers Ju 88s. Out of 115 bombers and 35 fighters the Luftwaffe sent over, 16 bombers and 7 fighters were shot down. Fighter Command Airfields in the North East escaped with only minimal damage, although the Bomber Command airfield at Driffield had several hangars destroyed. All in all, the mission was a disaster which became known as 'Black Thursday' and exposed the folly of conducting daylight bombing raids without adequate fighter escorts.

THE STARS OF THE SKIES:
Junkers Ju 88

The Junkers Ju 88 was the most successful of the Luftwaffe bombers used during The Battle of Britain, a fact borne out by the relative number of planes shot down in comparison to the slower and more cumbersome Dornier Do 17 or the various versions of the Heinkel He 111 deployed. Although part of this can be off-laid by the fact that fewer Ju 88s were deployed due to lingering teething problems with the design. Luftwaffe bomber pilots were also more accustomed to the heavier, slower bombers.

The Ju 88 was originally conceived as a twin-engine multi-purpose combat aircraft- or a *Schnellbomber* (fast bomber), a light frame aircraft that could use speed to avoid enemy fighter planes. During World War II, the Ju 88 was in constant production and became one of the Luftwaffe's most versatile aircraft. Originally designed as a 'dive-bomber' – a tactic much beloved by Luftwaffe pilots, the Ju 88 was quick enough to also act as a fighter-bomber, reconnaissance plane and even, towards the end of the war as a 'flying bomb'. The speed and versatility of the plane enabled it to roll in to steep dive and sweep manoeuvres to escape attacking RAF Hurricanes.

The production and technical issues limited the number of Ju 88s deployed during first period of The Battle of Britain but they,

Junker Ju 88

EXTRAORDINARY FACT

The founder of the Junkers aeronautical empire was an engineer named Hugo Junkers (1859–1935). Junkers, along with Russian born engineer Andrei Tupolev, were the first designers and pioneers of all-metal airframes. Junkers designed several aircraft used during World War I, but was more interested in designing aircraft for commercial and

Hugo Junkers

practical purposes rather than the production of war planes. When the Nazis came into power in 1933 they requested Junkers and his businesses' aid in the German re-armament programme. When Junkers – a known pacifist with socialist tendencies – declined, the Nazis responded by demanding ownership of all patents and market shares from his company and threatened Junkers with imprisonment on the grounds of High Treason. In 1934 Junkers was placed under house arrest, and died at home in 1935 during negotiations to give up the remaining stock and interests in Junkers. Under Nazi control, his company produced some of the most successful German warplanes of World War II.

nonetheless, took part in several notable raids on British ports and military and industrial complexes. There is an argument that if the technical issues had been resolved sooner and more Ju 88s available, this could have given the Luftwaffe a decisive advantage. The Ju 88 – with various modifications – continued to perform admirably throughout the war. A truly multi-dimensional war plane.

Junkers Ju 88 Specifications

Type: Fast Bomber (*Schnellbomber*) / Heavy Fighter / Dive Bomber
Crew: Up to 4
Length: 14.4 metres (47.2 ft)
Wingspan: 20 metres (65.6 ft)
Max Speed: 470 km/h (290 mph)
Range: 789.6 km (1,112 miles)
Armaments:
Guns: Up to 7 7.92 mm MG 81J mounted machine guns
Bombs: Up to 1,400 kilograms (3,100 lb) of ordnance internally in two bomb bays rated at 900 kg (2,000 lb) and 500 kg (1,100 lb) or up to 3,000 kg (6,600 lb) externally. Carrying bombs externally increased weight and drag and impaired the aircraft's performance.

Two aircraft Junkers Ju 88 on airfield at takeoff

WOMEN'S AUXILIARY AIRFORCE (WAAF)
The Key Role of Women in The Battle of Britain

The WAAF was first established in 1939 by King George VI. Auxiliary Territorial Service (ATS), the voluntary women's branch of the territorial army had been set up in 1938 but as preparations for war began, the British government decided that a separate women's air service was necessary. The WAAF was not, strictly speaking, a recognized wing of the RAF, but a separate organization interlinked with the RAF to provide personnel support at airfields and sector stations.

Initially the roles designated to the women of the WAAF were somewhat patronizing of their abilities and confined to domestic duties such as cooking and cleaning. Women were not permitted to fly aircraft, or even to train as pilots, although this changed in 1941 as more women were admitted to the Air Transport Auxiliary (see ATTA Girls page 71). However, during The Battle of Britain the RAF were under huge strain in terms of personnel and this resulted in a change of role for the WAAF. It became essential for the women of the organization to take on more technical roles, and they were trained in radar plotting, the maintenance of barrage balloons and photographic interpretation.

The role of the plotters at

WAAF poster

EXTRAORDINARY FACT

On 30 August RAF Biggin Hill suffered sustained damage from Luftwaffe bombing raids which claimed the lives of 39 people and destroyed aircraft hangars. The service staff who survived reported for duty the following day in an attempt to get the key airbase operable again. Two days later on 1 September the base was bombed again. WAAF staff Sergeant Joan Mortimer, Flight Officer Elspeth Henderson and Sergeant Helen Turner, all teleprinter operators, stayed at their posts during the raids as bombs fell all around them. Henderson and Mortimer were working in the Operations room which suffered a direct hit but continued to maintain contact with Fighter Command HQ until fire finally forced them to flee the building. Helen Turner even went out on to the airfield and marked unexploded bombs with red flags as the raid continued. All three women were awarded the Military Medal for their amazing bravery.

Sector Stations was of vital importance to Dowding's defence system. Radar reporters (often WAAF members) at Chain Home stations were entrusted with the task of detecting and reporting the positions of incoming air to Sector Control Rooms. It was then the job of the plotters to 'map' these raids and determine their likely targets and destinations. The plotters worked in teams of ten in three shifts to ensure full 24 hour coverage. When information was relayed from Radar Stations and the Observer Corps the plotters tracked the raids using wooden blocks placed on large maps on wooden tables. The blocks displayed the estimated size and strength of the raid, its likely target and were colour coded to indicate the time the information had been received, to ensure the information was as up to date as possible. Working with speed and accuracy was essential as lives of RAF pilots depended on the plotters so it was very much a high stress role performed in difficult conditions.

During the summer of 1940 the WAAFs used by Fighter Command numbered several thousand with personnel based at key Fighter Command airbases such as RAF Biggin Hill, Hawkinge and Manston. All three airbases were the target of Luftwaffe bombing raids during The Battle of Britain and the personnel were thereby putting their lives on hold while performing vital duties in tireless and brave service to their country. Without the support of the WAAF, Dowding's 'system' would most likely have faltered and failed to be as effective.

THE 'ATTA GIRLS'
Women Pilots and the Air Transport Auxiliary

The Air Transport Auxiliary (ATA) was a British civilian organization created in 1939 which had its headquarters at White Waltham Airfield in Berkshire. The role of the ATA was the transportation of new, recently repaired and damaged military aircraft between factories, assembly plants, maintenance units, active service squadrons and airfields. Other duties included providing an air taxi service for RAF personnel between airfields and bases and conducting air ambulance duties. One notable aspect was that ATA recruited female pilots, known as the 'ATTA Girls', with the first

The ATA had an innovative approach to equal opportunities many years ahead of its time. As the pilots were recruited from the civilian population they often accepted pilots who had been rejected by the RAF or Fleet Air Arm on the basis of age, physical fitness, gender and, perhaps most remarkably, physical disability. As long as they were able to effectively transport the aircraft, ATA contained amongst its ranks pilots with limbs missing, poor eye-sight and any number of other disabilities. This led to the often quoted 'joke' amongst the RAF that ATA stood for 'ancient and tattered airmen'. The ATA also recruited pilots from overseas, many volunteers from neutral countries. In total, representatives of 28 countries flew with the ATA during World War II. By 1943, the 'ATTA Girls', were granted equal pay with their male colleagues in recognition of the valuable role that they played – this was a notable 'first' for a British government organization.

women admitted into the service in January 1940.

Initially the ATA transported military personnel, the mail, food and medical supplies but by the start of The Battle of Britain it became clear that there was an urgent need to transport aircraft between factories and maintenance units as swiftly as possible. Initially, in order to comply with the Geneva Convention on the treatment of civilians during war time, the planes ATA transported were not fitted with armaments. However, after encounters with enemy patrols unaware the ferried aircraft were unarmed, the RAF began fitting all planes ATA transported with guns fully loaded. The exploits of the 'ATTA Girls' was a popular source of propaganda in the British press with several of the female pilots gaining pin-up status, notably Argentine born aviator Maureen Dunlop. In total 166 women pilots flew with ATA during World War II (1 in 8 of the overall cause) with 15 losing their lives to the cause.

At the end of the war an Air Pageant was held at ATA HQ at White Waltham Airfield to mark the disbanding of the service. Lord Beaverbrook, Minister for Air Production gave the following fitting tribute in his speech: 'Without the ATA the days and nights of The Battle of Britain would have been conducted under conditions quite different from the actual events. They carried out the delivery of aircraft from the factories to the RAF, thus relieving countless numbers of RAF pilots for duty in the battle. Just as The Battle of Britain is the accomplishment and achievement of the RAF, likewise it can be declared that the ATA sustained and supported them in the battle. They were soldiers fighting in the struggle just as completely as if they had been engaged on the battlefront.'

ATA pilot

'MISS SHILLING'S ORIFICE'
How Beatrice Shilling Solved the Problem of Engine Cut-Out

During The Battle of France and the early months of The Battle of Britain, RAF pilots discovered a flaw in the Rolls Royce Merlin engines that powered Spitfires and Hurricanes. During dogfights, when a pilot went into a nosedive manoeuvre, negative G-force caused fuel to flood the engine's carburettor, often leading the engine to cut out completely. German fighter planes were equipped with fuel injection engines that regulated the flow of fuel and so had a technical advantage over British planes. If a Luftwaffe pilot went into a steep dive manoeuvre pursuing a Spitfire or Hurricane, it could execute a half roll counter manoeuvre, but this was cumbersome and time consuming, sacrificing valuable seconds in the process. Although Rolls Royce hurriedly produced a modified and updated carburettor, this failed to solve the problem. It was left to an enterprising young RAF engineer named Beatrice Shilling (1909–1990) to find an innovative solution.

Beatrice Shilling was born in Waterlooville, Hampshire in 1909 and from an early age developed a keen interest in engineering. At the age of 14 she acquired a worn out Royal Enfield motorcycle which she renovated, teaching herself how each component part worked. On leaving school, Beatrice took up an apprenticeship with an electrical engineering company – an unusual career for a woman at the time, and worked for the company for three years. Beatrice's employer, Margaret Partridge, encouraged her to study for a degree in electrical engineering at The University of Manchester.

Shilling applied for a grant of £100 from The National Society for Women's Service, an organization born out of the suffragette movement, so that she could afford to pay the tuition fees.

On graduating, Beatrice found employment opportunities hard to come by, partly due to her gender but mainly due to the economic situation in Britain in the early 1930s. After conducting research into internal combustion engines and gaining a higher degree, Beatrice finally found employment with the Royal Aircraft Establishment (RAE), the research and development wing of the RAF based at Farnborough.

EXTRAORDINARY FACT

Beatrice 'Tilly' Shilling was a keen amateur motor racing enthusiast. In the 1930s she regularly raced her beloved Norton motorcycle at events at Brooklands racetrack in Surrey, often beating more established professional racers. 'Tilly' is one of only three women to be awarded the British Motorcycle Racing Clubs Gold Star, which was awarded to her for completing laps of Brooklands at speeds of over 100 mph. After the war, Beatrice switched to racing motor cars at race meets at Silverstone and Goodwood. Beatrice's first racing car was a Lagonda Rapier, which she modified to her own specifications in her home workshop and raced at member's meetings at Goodwood in the 1950s, recording several podium finishes. A collection of Tilly's race badges, trophies and other memorabilia of her racing career is housed at the Brooklands Motor Museum.

While at Farnborough, Beatrice became aware of the issues of engine cut-out during negative G-force manoeuvres and set about solving the problem. An acknowledged expert on internal combustion engines and talented physicist, Beatrice calculated that the problem could be relieved by restricting the flow of fuel to the engine when entering a dive. Beatrice designed a small, thimble like chamber that could be easily fitted to the engine which regulated fuel flow without sacrificing maximum engine power. Beatrice Shilling's 'restrictor' (nicknamed 'Miss Shilling's Orifice' by the pilots) was a revelation, and although was tested on only a dozen or so planes during The Battle of Britain, by March 1941 it had become a standard fitting on all Hurricanes and Spitfires.

DID YOU KNOW?

In 1967 Beatrice Shilling (aged 58) was invited to work as a technical consultant for the Formula One team 'All American Racing' by its owner Dan Gurney. The team had been having problems with Gurney's car, the Eagle Mk-1, most notably with sudden engine failure. Beatrice Shilling's engineering and mechanical expertise, coupled with her knowledge and enthusiasm for motor racing, made her the perfect candidate. Although Beatrice undoubtedly set about the task with her customary gusto and guile, making various modifications, she was unable to rectify the problem and advised that a design fault in the engine's fuel injection system was to blame. The Eagle Mk-1 was retired from Formula One racing at the end of the 1968 season.

DID YOU KNOW?

A handmade autograph book signed by over 100 Battle of Britain fighter pilots was sold in 2020 for £50,000 at auction. The book was originally put together by Norman Phillips, a mess steward at RAF Martlesham Heath in Suffolk. Phillips showed the book to Winston Churchill when he visited the airbase with Churchill proclaiming 'this isn't a book of names, it's a book of heroes, god-forbid it ever be lost'. Among 'the heroes' to sign the book were aces Robert Stanford Tuck and Douglas Bader, with the later allegedly making the covering of the book out of fabric he cut out of a chair in the officers' mess.

QUICK FACTS

• The altitude at which an RAF pilot was flying was measured in 'Angels'. One 'Angel' was equal to 1,000 feet (304.8 m) so if a pilot received instructions to 'climb to Angels 15' he was requested to ascend to 15,000 feet (4,572 m).

'THE HARDEST DAY': SUNDAY 18 AUGUST 1940
The Strain Shows On Both Sides

Although Adlertag had been unsuccessful, Albert Kesselring, the commander of Luftflotte 2 convinced Göring that the attacks on Fighter Command airfields should be sustained. Göring was becoming alarmed at the number of planes the Luftwaffe were losing on a daily basis but Kesselring offered a change of tactics. German intelligence had calculated that the RAF had less than 300 fighters at their disposal and coordinated attacks at specific targets in the South East of England would push Britain's air defences to breaking point. This was another example of faulty German intelligence as the RAF had close to 800 operational fighters with a further 300 in storage. Kesselring abandoned the previous strategy of scattered attacks all across the coast in favour of concentrated main raids on the sector stations at RAF Kenley, Biggin Hill, North Weald and Hornchurch, with secondary targets at RAF Ford, Gosport, Thorney Island and the Radar Station at Poling. The Luftwaffe persisted with their 'swarm' strategy of

AMAZING FACT

During 'The Hardest Day' the Luftwaffe scrambled 108 bombers and 150 fighter aircraft from their bases in Northern France and the Low Countries, finally taking to the air at 11 am, two hours later than scheduled. As the planes crossed Calais to rendezvous with fighter escorts, low level cloud made visibility tricky and the formations lost their unity and had to reform, losing more time. In the confusion some of the fighters had overtaken the bombers that were supposed to be ahead of them, meaning the plan of attack was now the wrong way round. The Dorniers that were supposed to attack first ended up 15 miles behind the other bombers.

Heinkel He III German Bombers

sending waves of fighters ahead to draw the RAF planes in to the aerial battles, believing that this weakened their airfield defences. After the disaster of 'Black Thursday' (see page 64) Göring issued orders that fighter escorts should fly in close formation to protect the bombers. Although this was intended to address the issue of Luftwaffe bomber losses (228 German planes had been shot down the previous week alone), it rendered the Messerschmitt Bf 109s less effective in dogfights.

★ AMAZING FACT ★

Although the British picked up the approaching enemy aircraft they over-estimated the strength of the German planes as approximately 350 aircraft, which was one-third more than the actual size of the force. As a result Dowding committed more planes to the air than he may have otherwise been inclined, scrambling a defence force of nine Squadrons from Number 11 Group with a further three reserve squadrons held at RAF Tangmere as reinforcements. Whereas the Luftwaffe under calculated RAF resources, ironically, the RAF did the opposite.

Between lunchtime and the evening, three main attack waves were launched by the Luftwaffe flying a total of 850 sorties and including a total of over 2,000 German airmen. RAF Kenley was badly damaged with its Sector Operations Room bombed and rendered inoperable (a back-up operations room was hurriedly set up in a nearby shop). Other German successes included severe damage to the runway and hangars RAF Ford and direct hits on the Home Chain Radar station at Poling. When low level cloud and mist descended in the early evening the Luftwaffe was forced to abandon their third wave of raids.

Sunday 18 August is known historically as 'The Hardest Day' as it saw the heaviest and most sustained aerial battles in a single day of the entire Battle of Britain. Both the RAF and the Luftwaffe incurred high numbers of aircraft casualties. Actual figures vary according to different sources (and over reporting of numbers by both sides) but an estimated 30 RAF Spitfires and Hurricanes were destroyed in the air with a further 39 damaged, and almost 30 aircraft were destroyed in airfield bombing raids. For their part the Luftwaffe lost around 70 aircraft, with a further 40 badly damaged, but suffered

Wreckage of Downed Dornier Bomber

considerably greater loss of personnel; Ten RAF pilots were killed with 20 wounded against 94 German airmen killed, 40 captured and many more wounded. In the final analysis, neither side could claim a significant victory as the losses to both sides were considerable and could not be sustained if battles of such ferocity were to continue at the same level. However, overall the RAF may have been slightly favoured in that they again managed to thwart the Luftwaffe raids despite being heavily outnumbered.

TOP GUNS AND FLYING ACES:
Paterson Clarence Hughes

Paterson 'Pat' Clarence Hughes (1917−1940) was born in the town of Cooma, New South Wales, Australia. As a boy, Hughes developed an obsession with aeroplanes, spending hours building models and homemade crystal radio sets and reading everything he could get his hands on about aviation. It was of little surprise when he enlisted with the Royal Australian Air Force (RAAF) in 1936 to train as a pilot at the age of 18. Hughes passed his basic Air Cadet training, although frequently was at odds with the

Paterson Clarence Hughes

rigours of RAAF discipline on account of his high-spirited personality and fondness for pranks. On graduation, Hughes applied to be transferred to the RAF and was accepted,

EXTRAORDINARY FACT

Pat Hughes was a larger than life character renowned amongst his fellow pilots for his love of practical jokes, unconventional flying methods and contempt for authority. When Hughes first transferred to the RAF he refused to exchange his dark blue RAAF uniform for the official RAF uniform of a different shade. Although eventually forced to relent, Hughes would often change back into his RAAF uniform before flying, believing that it brought him good luck.

Amongst the many stories of Hughes' eccentric behaviour, perhaps the most bizarre concerns his habit of taking his dog in the cockpit with him on flying missions. The dog was an Airedale terrier that Hughes named Flying Officer Butch and Hughes insisted that Butch was a tremendous asset to him and could sense approaching enemy planes. Hughes' superiors were not impressed and barred him from taking Butch on missions. Legend has it that when news of Hughes' death came through, the dog ran out of the officer's mess and was never seen again.

QUICK FACTS

• Hughes had an unconventional technique when engaged in dog-fights, one which ultimately led to his downfall. At the start of The Battle of Britain it was accepted Fighter Command strategy to fire upon the enemy from a distance (around 200 yards), a tactic that proved ineffectual. By August, Hughes would close on his targets to a distance of around 30 yards, often engaging his targets head on in a game of 'chicken'.

arriving in England in 1937.

In contrast to his time with the RAAF, Hughes excelled in England, rapidly completing his advanced pilot training and joining No. 64 Squadron based at RAF Church Fenton in Yorkshire. Hughes initially flew Bristol Blenheims, but after being promoted to flight lieutenant he transferred to No. 234 Squadron and began flying Spitfires by the time that war broke out in 1939.

At the start of The Battle of Britain, No. 234 Squadron were relocated to RAF St Eval in Cornwall as part of No. 10 Group. It was not long before Hughes was in the thick of the action claiming his first aerial victories by shooting down two German Junkers Ju 88 over Land's End on 8 July. At the height of The Battle of Britain, Hughes' Squadron were relocated again to RAF Middle Wallop in Hampshire. During the most intense periods of the Battle between August 15 and 18, Hughes shot down six Messerschmitt Bf 109s and a further two on 28 August.

Hughes was killed in action on 7 September when intercepting and shooting down a Dornier Do 17 bomber en-route to London. It is thought that Hughes' habit of

Medals awarded to Pat Hughes

getting close up to his targets resulted in his Spitfire becoming damaged by debris from the stricken German plane. Other eyewitness accounts claim that the guns on Hughes' Spitfire had either jammed or had run out of ammunition and he

EXTRAORDINARY FACT

Although Battle of Britain folklore is littered with countless stories of amazing courage and bravery, only one of 'the Few' was ever awarded The Victoria Cross. That distinction belongs to James Brindley Nicholson of No. 249 Squadron.

On 16 August, during the height of the Luftwaffe's *Adlertag* offensive, Flight Lieutenant Nicholson was scrambled in his Hawker Hurricane from RAF Boscombe Down when he came under fire from a Messerschmitt Bf 109. Nicholson was badly injured in the attack and his Fighter's fuel tank set on fire. Just as Nicholson prepared to bail out, he spotted another Bf 109 which he pursued and managed to shoot down despite his cockpit being engulfed in flames.

Nicholson was eventually able to escape from the cockpit and parachute to safety but suffered severe burns to his hands, face and neck and the loss of sight in one eye. After a period of convalescence, Nicholson re-joined the RAF and took up a post in India, eventually rising to the rank of Wing Commander. Sadly, despite his heroics, James Nicholson did not survive the war and was killed in an aircraft accident on 2 May 1945 when the plane he was travelling in malfunctioned and caught fire before crashing into the Bay of Bengal.

deliberately rammed the German bomber. Hughes bailed out but either his parachute failed to open, or he lost consciousness as his body was found on the ground several miles from his wrecked Spitfire. In total Hughes recorded 17 aerial victories, the majority of which came during the most intense period of the conflict, making him the highest scoring Australian ace of The Battle of Britain and the joint second highest Australian airman of World War II. Pat Hughes was posthumously awarded the Distinguished Flying Cross for bravery.

QUICK FACTS

• A flying ace, fighter ace or air ace is a military aviator, usually a fighter pilot, credited with shooting down several enemy aircraft during aerial combat. The actual number of aerial victories required to officially qualify as an ace has varied, but it is usually considered to be five or more. Use of the term 'ace' to describe these pilots began in World War I, when French newspapers coined the term 'Les As' (the ace) to describe Adolphe Pégoud, after he became the first pilot to down five German aircraft. The British initially used the term 'star-turns' (a show business term), while the Germans described their elite fighter pilots as *Überkanonen* (which roughly translates to 'top guns').

TOP GUNS AND FLYING ACES:
Heinrich Bär

Heinrich Bär (1913−1957) held the distinction of serving the Luftwaffe on all major German theatres of war flying missions on the Mediterranean, Eastern and Western fronts with a total score of more than a thousand combat sorties. Amazingly Bär was shot down 18 times and was seriously wounded three times and survived. Bär was a Saxon, proud of his thick accent, who joined the Reichswehr in 1934 and transferred to the Luftwaffe in 1935. Initially serving as a mechanic, he learned to fly transport aircraft prior to training as a fighter pilot. Bär achieved his first aerial victory on the French border in a skirmish during 'the phoney war' of September 1939.

During the Battle of Britain, Bär is credited with downing 17 RAF fighter planes. On 2 September 1940 Bär's plane was shot down by a Spitfire over the English Channel, causing Bär to bail out and he was eventually rescued from the sea by a passing German U-Boat. Bär was summoned to appear before Hermann Göring and provide a report on the mission. When Göring asked Bär what he was thinking about while in the water, Bär immediately replied, 'Your speech, Herr *Reichsmarschall*, in which you said that England is no longer an island!' alluding to an address that Göring had made before the German fighter pilots. Such incidents are examples of Bär's often blatant disregard for higher authority with his outspokenness frequently landing him in trouble with Göring.

When the invasion of the Soviet Union started, Bär was transferred to the Eastern Front, where he accumulated further kills including gaining 'ace in a day' status by downing six

Soviet aircraft on the 30 August 1941. In February 1942, Bär was awarded the Knight's Cross of the Iron Cross with Oak Leaves and Swords despite Göring attempting to block the award on the grounds of Bär's rebellious attitude. During the last years of the war, Bär also flew in the Messerschmitt Me 262 jet fighter, claiming 17 victories in an aircraft notoriously difficult to fly.

At the end of the war on May 4, 1945, Bär ordered his pilots to surrender, after destroying their Messerschmitt ME 262 jets. This decision was not taken lightly by his commanding officers and he was almost shot for insubordination. He avoided the firing squad, surrendered, and survived the war. In total Bar was responsible for 220 aerial victories over allied aircraft during World War II. After the war, Bär continued his career as an aviator, working as a consultant and test pilot for sports aviation companies. Heinrich Bär was killed while testing a sports aircraft on 26 April 1957 when his plane malfunctioned and crashed at an airfield in Brunswick, Germany.

Messerschmitt Me 262

TOP GUNS AND FLYING ACES:
Werner Mölders

Werner Mölders

Werner Mölders (1913–1941) was one of the leading Luftwaffe aces during The Battle of Britain, with his logbook recording that he took part in 238 combat missions and 71 reconnaissance flights between July 1940 and March 1941. Mölders originally trained as an infantry officer but volunteered to train as a pilot. Initially Mölders request was turned down as he failed to pass suitability tests. Mölders suffered from air-sickness and vertigo but managed to overcome these afflictions and passed his pilot training and joined the newly created Luftwaffe in 1935.

In 1936, Hitler sent The Condor Legion, a military force of the German army and air force, to fight for the nationalists in the Spanish civil war. Mölders volunteered for service and was placed under the command of Adolf Galland (see page 94). Mölders excelled during the conflict in Spain and became the leading ace of the Condor Legion, claiming 16 aerial victories.

When World War II broke out, Mölders served in the Battle of France and continued his prolific record of combat victories. By June 1940, Mölders is credited with shooting down 20 Allied aircraft and damaging countless more, earning him The Knight's Cross of The Iron Cross. On 5 June 1940, whilst undertaking his 133rd combat mission of the war,

While fighting in the Spanish Civil War, Werner Mölders developed a new combat formation for fighters known as 'the four finger' formation. Fighters lined up and flew in unison, spaced out like the fingers of an outstretched hand. The four finger formation enabled a wider field of vision and enhanced protection and was the standard strategy adopted by the Luftwaffe in The Battle of Britain.

Mölders' Messerschmitt Bf109 was shot down over northern France. Mölders managed to bail out but was captured by French troops as a prisoner of war. Mölders was initially harshly treated by his captors who beat him and stole his Knight's Cross medal. Mölders only spent three weeks in captivity as the armistice of France was signed on 24 June 1940 and he was released. There is an apocryphal story that a French soldier was later sentenced to death for beating Mölders in captivity but Mölders petitioned Göring on his behalf and the sentence was overturned.

Mölders resumed his duties with the Luftwaffe, having been

Jagdgeschwader 51 Squadron

Heinkel He 111

promoted to the rank of major and put in command of *Jagdgeschwader* 51 (JG-51) one of the air forces crack fighter squadrons. Between late July 1940 and the 1 December there were 31 recorded aerial victories in The Battle of Britain, to add to a tally of 25 in the Battle of France. When Mölders was recalled from duty over the channel front to help prepare for the impending invasion of the Soviet Union in February 1941, he had recorded a total of 68 victories.

Mölders was awarded a second Knight's Cross and promoted to the rank of *Oberst* (Colonel) which effectively barred him from flying combat missions. It has been speculated by some historians that such was Mölders' celebrity (he was a valuable asset in German war propaganda) that he was too valuable to risk losing in active service. Mölders took up a strategic planning role on the Eastern Front and was killed in an air accident when the Heinkel He 11 he was travelling in on a flight between Germany and Crimea crashed during a thunderstorm. Werner Mölders was given a state funeral with Göring giving the eulogy. He was 28 years old.

THE 303 SQUADRON
Polish Pilots In The Battle of Britain

In the aftermath of the German invasion of Poland in September 1939, many Polish military personnel escaped first to France, where they fought against the German invasion, and then subsequently to Britain. By June 1940, 8,000 Polish airmen were seeking sanctuary on British soil and on 11 June 1940 an agreement was signed between the government and the Polish government in exile to form the Polish Airforce in Britain. In July 1940, Squadron 302 and Squadron 303 were formed of Polish fighter pilots and ground crew. Initially RAF commanders were sceptical of the Polish fighter's worth to the Allied cause. This was partly due to a suspicion that the Poles defeat at the hands of the Luftwaffe was evidence of ineffectiveness in battle, but mainly it was the language barrier as many of the pilots spoke little or no English.

The Polish pilots undertook intensive training in English language and RAF strategy and Fighter Command codes.

The 303 Squadron was nicknamed 'Kościuszko' after the 18th century Polish-American military hero Tadeusz Kościuszko who fought as a brigadier general in the American Revolutionary War. Kościuszko was a close friend of Thomas Jefferson and in his will stipulated that his assets should be used to fund the education and emancipation of American slaves.

EXTRAORDINARY FACT

Many of the Polish pilots of 303 Squadron had fought the Luftwaffe in Europe and were highly skilled in dogfights. The Polish pilots were reticent to follow the rigid formations and battle strategies of the RAF and often improvised, preferring to engage the enemy planes with close up attacks. One story that illustrates the Polish penchant for spontaneity in battle concerns 303's Sgt Stanislaw Karubin, who adopted extreme tactics to bring down a Messerschmitt Bf 109. After a lengthy dog fight, Karubin was tailing the German fighter at low altitude. Just as he closed in for the kill, Sgt Karubin noticed that his Hurricane had run out of ammunition. Instead of aborting the battle and returning to safety, Karubin flew directly above the Bf 109, causing its pilot to panic and forcing the German plane to crash into the trees below. Low altitude combat and close fire engagement were hallmarks of the Polish fighters' battle strategy and later in the war the 303 developed these tactics to great effect in ground attacks known as 'rhubarb' sorties.

It quickly became apparent that far from being inept, the Polish fighters were highly skilled veterans with hundreds of flying hours behind them and invaluable combat experience, something that their British counterparts lacked. On the 30 August 1940, 303 Squadron were carrying out training manoeuvres over Hertfordshire when they encountered an escorted German bomber formation. Although the squadron was not officially operational, Flying Officer Ludwik

Paszkiewicz defied orders to remain in tight formation and sent his Hurricane in pursuit of a Messerschmitt Bf 109 that he duly shot down. F/O Paszkiewicz was initially reprimanded for failing to follow orders by his British commanding officer R G Kellet, who simultaneously congratulated the pilot for claiming the squadron's first victory. 303 Squadron was pronounced fully operational with immediate effect the following day.

Ludwik Paszkiewicz

The 303 Squadron quickly made a name for themselves as one of the crack squadrons of The Battle of Britain. Between

303 Squadron

the 31 August and 11 October 1940, when the squadron was moved from RAF Northolt for a well-earned rest, 303 Squadron shot down 126 enemy aircraft in little over six weeks. The top Polish aces were Flying Officer Witold Urbanowicz with 17 aerial victories. Flying Officer Antoni Glowacki also held the distinction of being one of only two Allied pilots to gain 'ace in a day' status by downing five enemy plans on 24 August. In total, 303 Squadron boasted five pilots with ace status, four of whom were awarded the Distinguished Flying Medal, and it was the highest scoring Hurricane squadron by some distance. Sir Hugh Dowding wrote 'Had it not been for the magnificent skills contributed by the Polish squadrons and their unsurpassed gallantry, I hesitate to say that the outcome of the Battle (of Britain) would have been the same.'

TOP GUNS AND FLYING ACES:
Adolf Galland

Adolf Josef Ferdinand Galland (1912–1996) was already a seasoned fighter pilot prior to the commencement of The Battle of Britain, receiving the Iron Cross First Class in May 1940 for his heroism in the skies over France and Belgium.

Starting his flying career as a glider pilot in 1929, he joined the German army and was sent to the Baltic Sea to train on flying boats before joining the ZVS (Central Airline Pilot School) where, as part of his training, he flew commercial planes for Lufthansa, and trained as a fighter pilot with the Italian Air Force, eventually joining Göring's Luftwaffe in 1933.

In 1937, during the Spanish Civil War, Galland was sent to support Franco's Nationalists, receiving the Spanish Cross at the end of the conflict for his contribution to their victory. He then became a test pilot before providing, at the outbreak of World War II, air support to the German army during the invasion of Poland, whereupon he received the Iron Cross Second Class for flying nearly 360 missions in two wars and averaging two missions per day.

Adolf Galland

He was subsequently transferred to Jagdgeschwader 27 (JG 27—Fighter Wing 27) in February when (the already recognized flying ace) Werner Mölders, gave him the opportunity to join his unit and gave him guidance around leadership in the air, tactics and organization, which he put to good use during the invasion

DID YOU KNOW?

Galland always had deep respect for the British flying aces, and became lifelong friends with Group Captain Douglas Bader and Wing Commander Robert Stanford Tuck. In fact, when, on separate occasions, they were both shot down over France he invited them to dinner before they were taken off to a prison camp.

*Diamonds of his
Knight's Cross*

of the Low Countries, France and the Battle for Belgium during May 1940.

Having been promoted to major, Galland saw his first action during The Battle of Britain in July 1940 and swiftly notched up seventeen victories, flying two to three sorties a day, for which he was awarded the Knight's Cross, and then, only six weeks later, with his tally having risen to forty, he became only the third Luftwaffe pilot to win the Oak Leaves to his Knight's Cross.

Galland was reported to have been very impressed with the speed and manoeuvrability of the British Spitfire, as well as the tenacity and courage shown by his RAF adversaries, who were inflicting heavy losses on the Luftwaffe.

On 18 August Galland was summoned to a meeting with Göring to review tactics and this proved to be the first of many disagreements between the two men. Göring insisted that Galland's fighters should provide a close escort to their slow-moving bombers which flew at medium altitudes, which perfectly suited the Spitfire. Galland felt that fighter pilots should have the freedom to roam and engage the enemy on their own terms but Göring would not move his position on this, despite Galland's claim that the morale of his pilots was being affected by having to undertake close-escort missions. On his return to action (22 August) Galland replaced Gotthard Handrick as commander of JG26 and immediately replaced the group and squadron commanders that he considered to be ineffective with younger and more hard-hitting officers and, unlike his predecessor, flew as many

EXTRAORDINARY FACT

It is remarkable that Adolf Galland ever became a flying ace at all as his eyesight was impaired due to crash landing a biplane in 1935. He was unconscious for three days and sustained eye damage, a fractured skull and a broken nose. On recovery, he was declared unfit for flying but a friend managed to keep the doctor's report secret and he somehow managed to continue flying. However, when he was hospitalized again in 1936, the original medical report was discovered and he was grounded. Desperate to get back in the air, Galland admitted having fragments of glass in his eye but succeeded in convincing medical staff that he was fit to fly, on the condition that he underwent eye tests. By some means, one of his brothers managed to get hold of the eyecharts that were to be used, allowing Galland to memorize them and pass the test with flying colours.

missions as possible and led from the front during the most difficult operations.

As German bomber losses mounted up, Göring became increasingly critical of his fighter pilots and in a briefing of front line general officers on Luftwaffe tactics he asked what his fighter pilots required to win the battle, to which Galland replied, to Göring's fury, 'I should like an outfit of Spitfires for my squadron'.

After The Battle of Britain Galland remained based in France and by November 1941 his tally had risen to 94. When Werner Mölders was killed in a crash on 21 November, Galland was promoted to major general at the age of thirty, becoming the youngest general officer in the German armed forces, and was presented with the Diamonds of his Knight's Cross, personally by Hitler.

As the war progressed, Galland tried hard to improve tactics and morale but the Allied onslaught was taking its toll and in 1944 Galland reported that the Luftwaffe had lost over 1,000 day time pilots between January and April. Hitler and Göring were now focussing on the development of pilotless

DID YOU KNOW?

Galland acted as a technical adviser for the 1969 film *Battle of Britain*, along with his friend and old adversary, Robert Stanford Tuck, the character Major Falke being based on Galland himself. There were several disputes between Galland and the director during filming – he was upset that the director had decided not to use real names; he objected to a planned sequence involving him giving a Nazi salute to Göring, which he demanded was written out, and even bringing his lawyer to the studio at one point; and he became angry at the way the Germans were being portrayed in a stereotypical manner, again insisting that some scenes were re-written. Sir Michael Caine, one of the stars of the film, wrote in his biography that there were severe arguments with the former Luftwaffe pilot and that Galland had maintained that the Luftwaffe did not really lose The Battle of Britain.

revenge weapons (V1 buzz bomb and V2 rocket) which they were convinced would force the British to surrender and they blamed Galland's tactics for the collapse of the German fighter division.

The V-1 flying bomb

Galland led an attack against a formation of American bombers over Munich on 26 April, 1945, and crash landed, badly injuring his knee. He was captured and subsequently spent two years in a prison camp.

Upon release, Galland went on to become a successful aviation consultant, spending six years in Argentina and, as a fluent Spanish speaker, he lectured and trained pilots of the Argentinian air force. He returned to Bonn in 1957 and started his own successful aircraft consultancy. He died on 9 February 1996 aged 84.

THE BIG WING CONTROVERSY:
RAF In-Fighting During The Battle of Britain

Most patriotic histories of The Battle of Britain portray it as a stunning victory against all the odds by 'the few' over the mighty 'many' of the Luftwaffe. Although there is no doubting the unbelievable bravery of RAF fighter command pilots and the sacrifices endured in the process, what is often overlooked is the tensions within Fighter Command itself. One such area of contention is the 'Big Wing' controversy which caused considerable strain at the height of the battle and arguably led to the removal of Hugh Dowding as Air Chief Marshall.

'The Big Wing' was a tactic for aerial battle devised by Douglas Bader and Trafford Leigh Mallory, the commander of Group 12 Mallory and Bader believed that the only way to defeat the Luftwaffe comprehensively was to fight fire with fire and send up 'Big Wing' patrols of multiple squadrons to engage the enemy with as much fire-power as could be mustered. Dowding however, vehemently disagreed, believing it was important to preserve RAF resources as much as possible for what may turn out to be a battle of attrition. Dowding also argued that most RAF airfields were not equipped to launch large scale formations of squadrons simultaneously so this would mean scrambling planes in phases which would lose valuable time. The Big Wing formations would have to be formed once all the planes were airborne and by the time of the rendezvous many German bomber units would be at their targets. In addition, the time delay would also have a profound effect upon the advantages that Dowding's air defence system gained from information

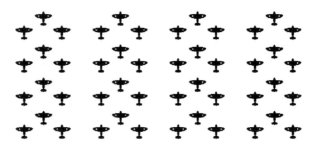

'Big Wing' formation of four squadrons

provided by radar stations.

One possible reason for the dispute however, was simple professional jealousy. Leigh Mallory is thought to have been livid when Dowding turned his request down to command the Group No. 11 and appointed the prestigious role to Keith Park whom Mallory despised. As a result, Mallory set about under-mining Dowding's orders by actively encouraging his side-kick Bader to behave insubordinately whilst simultaneously sowing discontent with Dowding's tactics with his friends and contacts at the Air Ministry. At the end of The Battle of Britain, Dowding was replaced as Air Chief Marshall by Sholto Douglas, a key ally of Mallory, who promptly sacked Keith Park as commander of Group No. 11, replacing him with Mallory.

Although Leigh Mallory 'won' his internal battle with Dowding and Park, it is generally accepted that Dowding's tactics and opposition to the Big Wing was the correct approach. For one thing, the use of light squadrons on interceptor missions allowed for rapid responses to raids and fooled the Luftwaffe into believing that the RAF's resources were more depleted than they really were.

THE NERVE CENTRE OF NO. 11 GROUP
The Operations Bunker at RAF Uxbridge

The vital nerve centre of No. 11 Group was the Operations Room at RAF Uxbridge which was hurriedly constructed in 1939 on the eve of the outbreak of war. Hugh Dowding predicted that in order to disable Britain's air defences, the Luftwaffe would target RAF airfields and that it was essential to have Operations Rooms that were virtually impregnable to German Bombing raids.

RAF Uxbridge was chosen as the site for No 11 Group and Dowding proposed building the Operations Room below ground in a bunker. Initial excavations took place in 1938 with construction taking place between February and August 1939 with the paint still drying on the walls when war broke out.

The bunker was built by the civilian construction company McAlpine and undertaken in secret with construction workers required to sign the Official Secrets Act to keep the location of the Operations Room from falling in to enemy hands.

The base of the bunker was 18.29 m (60 ft) below ground and was accessed by a staircase of 76 steps. The walls, floor and ceiling were constructed of 1 metre (3.28 feet) thick reinforced concrete with waterproofing to prevent flooding. All necessary utilities into and out of the building, such as electricity, water, telephone lines, heating, air filtration system and sewage were channelled along an intricate system of pipes running down the staircase. The solid concrete walls and the approximately 9.14 m (30 ft) of earth above the bunker's ceiling meant that it was safe from even the most powerful German armaments. The bunker consisted of a main operational room, the offices for the Air Vice Marshall (Sir Keith Park) and his staff, a separate annexe for the intelligence services and other amenities to serve the sixty operatives who worked tirelessly around the clock in eight-hour shifts. The bunker also contained a VIP room/Royal Box. King George VI and wife Queen Elizabeth made an undercover trip to inspect the facilities and meet the staff, while Winston Churchill made several top-secret trips to the bunker. Churchill visited the bunker on 16 August 1940 and is said to have spoken the famous words 'Never in the field of human conflict was so much owed, by so many, to so few'. Churchill

No.11 Group Operations Room in the "Battle of Britain Bunker" at RAF Uxbridge

was visibly impressed by the diligence, courage and fortitude of Fighter Command and uttered the phrase as he was leaving the bunker by car. The phrase became the keynote of his speech to the House of Commons on 20 August 1940.

Following the Luftwaffe's decision to begin an all-out bombing campaign on London in September 1940, Churchill made a surprise visit to the bunker on 15 September. In his memoirs, Churchill describes the moment during his visit when 'all of the bulbs glowed red', referring to the squadron state boards in the Operations Room which indicated that every No. 11 Group squadron was engaged in combat at the same time. Churchill is reported to have turned to Keith Park and asked how many pilots and planes No. 11 Group had in reserve. Park replied 'None, I'm putting in our last'. Park later wrote that Churchill went very pale and 'looked quite grave'.

The role of the Operations Bunker at RAF Uxbridge was instrumental in Fighter Command repelling the Luftwaffe. The bunker has been preserved as a lasting monument to the people (mostly women) who worked long hours underground in stressful situations and it is now open to the public as a museum.

COTTON'S CLUB
How Sidney Cotton's Photographs Revealed the Locations of Key Targets

Frederick Sidney Cotton OBE (1894–1969) was an Australian inventor, photographer and aviation and photography pioneer, who developed an early colour film process, and was largely accountable for the development of photographic reconnaissance before and during World War II.

Appointed as a Squadron Leader and honorary Wing Commander in 1939, Cotton was recruited to head up RAF 1 Photographic Development Unit (PDU) at Heston Aerodrome. This unit provided important intelligence which lead to successful air raids on key enemy installations. With his experience and knowledge, Cotton greatly improved the RAF's photo reconnaissance capabilities. The PDU was originally equipped with Bristol Blenheims, but Cotton considered these unsuitable, and slow, and he consequently obtained some Supermarine Spitfires, which were then steadily adapted to fly higher and faster. With a special blue, highly polished surface, known as PRU Blue, and camouflage scheme developed by Cotton himself, the modified engines produced more power at high altitudes. Under his leadership, the 1 PDU acquired the nickname 'Cotton's Club'.

Cotton's aerial photographs were far ahead of their time. Together with other members of the 1 PDU, he pioneered the techniques of high-altitude, high-speed stereoscopic photography that were instrumental in revealing the locations of many crucial military and intelligence targets. His photographs were used to establish the size and the characteristic launching mechanisms for the V-1 flying bomb and the V-2 rocket. Cotton also worked on ideas such as a prototype specialist reconnaissance aircraft and further refinements of photographic equipment.

Cotton died on 13 February 1969 aged 74 and was later memorialised in the name of the Sidney Cotton Bridge, on the O'Connell River, south of Proserpine, Queensland.

Part Four: Rage In The Skies

After a few weeks of relatively light combat, The Battle of Britain entered a new and vital phase on 30 August 1940. Hitler had become increasingly impatient with the inability of the Luftwaffe to strike critical blows to disable Britain's air defences. The invasion of Britain had initially been scheduled for early September and any further delays would mean abandoning Operation Sea Lion due to possible inclement weather conditions.

GÖRING HITS THE SECTOR STATIONS
30 / 31 August 1940

On 30 August Göring launched a huge series of waves on RAF sector stations and airfields with the first raid sweeping across Kent and Sussex at 10.30 am with second and third wave attacks throughout the afternoon and evening. Group No. 11 bore the brunt of the battle, backed up by reinforcements from Group No. 12. In total Fighter Command flew 1,054 sorties with a then record twenty-two squadrons engaged. Airfields at Biggin Hill, Kenley and North Weald were targeted, with Biggin Hill suffering the worst damage with one of its main hangars completely destroyed and telephone and electricity lines put out of action.

The Luftwaffe continued the all-out assault the following day on 31 August with airfields at RAF Duxford, Croydon and Hornchurch targeted and Biggin Hill bombed for the second day running. Fighter Command suffered their heaviest losses of The Battle of Britain with 39 aircraft shot down and 14 pilots killed. The Luftwaffe losses were also considerable, losing 38 aircraft during the onslaught that also targeted Chain Low and Chain Low Home radar stations (British early warning radar systems

RAF Duxford Airfield

operated by the RAF). Although Biggin Hill again suffered considerable damage to its telephone lines (which had only just been repaired from the previous day's raids), remarkably it was still able to operate by the late afternoon. The repeated attacks on Biggin Hill did have a cumulative effect however and forced Keith Park to remove two of the three squadrons based there to other satellite airfields.

REVENGE ATTACKS:
The Luftwaffe Change Tactics

One aspect often debated by historians is the sudden change in emphasis adopted by the Luftwaffe in September 1940 when attention was switched away from raids on airfields in favour of large-scale raids on London and other cities. It is certainly true that the intensity of the German raids on RAF ground installations and airfields at the end of August and beginning of September were starting to take their toll on

EXTRAORDINARY FACT

Hitler was initially against the bombing of civilian areas. On 1 August 1940, Hitler issued 'Directive No. 17' that stated London was not to be bombed without his explicit permission but reserved the right to adopt 'terror attack' measures as a means of retaliation and reprisal. Preparations for such an eventuality were drawn up under the codename Operation Loge (Loge being the German codename for London). The main focus however was to target communications, power stations, armaments factories and the Port of London, residential areas were not to be targeted deliberately, but any civilian casualties would undoubtedly have an indirect effect upon British morale.

Fighter Command's resources and morale. Although in terms of aircraft and pilots lost and aerial battles won, the numbers on both sides were often more-or-less even, the Luftwaffe's vast resources meant that such attritional warfare was probably hurting the RAF to a greater degree. Furthermore, the relentlessness of the German raids gave little recovery time for Fighter Command to regroup, repair and replace damaged aircraft and airfields.

Although RAF Bomber Command had been running small scale raids on cities in Germany since the beginning of The Battle of Britain, these had caused minimal damage. On 25 August however, Bomber Command dispatched 80 bombers on a raid to Berlin, primarily to bomb industrial targets. However, poor visibility made it difficult to accurately identify the intended targets and the bombers were forced to drop bombs indiscriminately, hitting residential areas and causing civilian casualties. This enraged Hitler, who interpreted it as a deliberate terror attack and promptly withdrew his directive (see box) that London should not be bombed. On 4 September Hitler gave an impassioned speech condemning the bombing of Berlin and vowing immediate reprisals in retaliation. On 3 September Göring (who was now stationed in France having

Bombed streets in Berlin

previously conducted his battle plans from his hunting lodge headquarters at Carinhall) convened a conference with his senior commanders. It was decided to switch emphasis away from airfields and aircraft production factories and unleash an all-out assault on London. The Luftwaffe had received intelligence that Fighter Command squadrons had been reduced to no more than five to seven aircraft each and that the attacks on the airfields had caused widespread infrastructure damage. Göring was persuaded by Albert Kesselring that the assault on London would draw out Fighter Command's reserves but interestingly Hugo Sperrle, commander of Luftflotte 3, urged caution, believing, quite correctly, that the assessment of Fighter Command strength was inaccurate and the assaults on airfields should continue. Sperrle was over-ruled and a mass attack was planned for 7 September under the codename *Vergeltungsangriff* (revenge attack).

THE BLITZ BEGINS: 7 SEPTEMBER 1940
London in the Firing Line

The 7 September marked the beginning of the final phase of The Battle of Britain and the change in Luftwaffe strategy – which proved to be a turning point. The day began in similar fashion to the previous few weeks with the Luftwaffe running light reconnaissance sorties. When this wasn't followed up by a first wave daylight raid, Fighter Command became suspicious that a full-scale assault was imminent and squadrons were placed on full alert. Historical

Extensive bomb and blast damage to Hallam Street and Duchess Street during the Blitz, Westminster, London May 1940

EXTRAORDINARY FACT

During a raid on London on 12 September 1940, a time-delayed bomb landed perilously close to St Paul's Cathedral. Miraculously the 2,000-kilogram (4,410 lb) bomb failed to detonate and was successfully defused and removed by a bomb disposal detachment of Royal Engineers under the command of Lieutenant Robert Davies. The bomb had landed in soft soil adjacent to the cathedral and had it detonated, it would have totally destroyed the cathedral. It took three days to dig the bomb out of the ground, work made even more perilous by a fire at a fractured gas main nearby. Davies and his team placed the recovered bomb on a lorry, which was driven to Hackney Marshes, where the bomb was safely detonated, leaving a crater 100 feet (30 m) wide. In recognition of their bravery, Davies and his assistant, Sapper George Wylie, were each awarded the George Cross.

records show that the first information passed from Chain Home Stations began filtering through to Bentley Priory HQ around mid-afternoon. It quickly became apparent that Fighter Command's suspicions were correct and that Göring had launched a vast airborne armada of over 1,000 aircraft.

Dowding and Park estimated that London must be the target of such a large show of force and rapidly scrambled a defence force of 11 squadrons from Group No. 11 with additional back-up from Group No. 12. The battles above London were ferocious and raged throughout the afternoon and late in to the night. The primary targets were the docks

DID YOU KNOW?

One of the most negative aspects of the Luftwaffe's change in strategy and of targeting London were the longer distances their fighters were required to fly in comparison to targeting coastal airfields. The Messerschmitt Bf 109E escorts had a limited fuel capacity resulting in only a 660 km (410 mile) maximum range solely on internal fuel. This dramatically reduced their effectiveness as when they reached their targets they had only an estimated 10 minutes of combat time before having to return to base. This often meant having to leave the bombers undefended by escorts and therefore vulnerable.

Messerschmitt Bf 109E

Firemen at work in a bomb damaged street in London,
after a Saturday night raid, circa 1941

in the east end of London but the Luftwaffe dropped their
bombs over a wide-area causing huge plumes of smoke to
billow into the air over London. The first day of the Blitz
was costly, causing the deaths of over 300 civilians with many
hundreds more injured and widespread damage to the docks
and power stations. In addition, the RAF lost 15 Spitfires and
17 Hurricanes (with 11 pilots killed, including Australian Ace
Pat Hughes, see page 81). The Luftwaffe, for their part, lost
38 aircraft in total and duly claimed the day as a victory with
the Nazi propaganda machine reporting London to be ablaze.
Keith Park flew his personal Hurricane over the still smoking
city the following day to assess the damage. Park later wrote
that although it was a distressing sight, he felt oddly relieved
as he knew then that the Luftwaffe were no longer targeting
airfields and this would provide his exhausted pilots with
much needed respite and recovery time.

THE BATTLE OF BRITAIN MOVIE (1969)
The Making of the Iconic War Film

The 1969 film *The Battle of Britain* was the brainchild of film producers S. Benjamin Fisz and Harry Saltzman. Originally Fisz had been planning a bio-pic of British Army hero Orde Wingate, but ran in to legal issues with the Wingate family. Originally from Poland, Fisz had flown with the RAF during World War II and a visit to his former air base gave him the idea of making a film about The Battle of Britain. Fisz and Saltzman enlisted Guy Hamilton as director, who Saltzman had worked with previously on James Bond films. Hamilton, a known stickler for details, envisaged the film as an accurate dramatization of the historic battle and wanted to move away from the propaganda style of earlier British war films. To this end, Douglas Bader, James Lacey, Robert Stanford Tuck, Adolf Galland (see page 94) and Sir Hugh Dowding were employed as technical consultants to ensure historical accuracy.

Hamilton also wanted the flying scenes to appear as authentic as possible and to minimize the use of models in the special effects. In order to achieve the desired look, Fisz and Saltzman began acquiring aircraft from the RAF to use in the filming. In total, over a hundred aircraft took part in the air battle sequences supported by radio-controlled models and other non-airworthy planes for set dressing.

Although several British airfields and RAF bases were used as locations, (most notably RAF Duxford where a disused aircraft hangar was blown up during the Eagle Day sequences), due to the vagaries of British weather, sequences were also filmed at air bases in Malta and Spain. The use of real aircraft

During The Battle of Britain only Mk1 and Mk2 Spitfires were deployed. Unfortunately the producers could only locate one Mk1 Spitfire that was air worthy enough to use in filming. All of the other Spitfires seen on screen are actually later versions of the Supermarine Spitfire which were modified to look like planes of Battle of Britain vintage. For the German aircraft, the producers acquired 17 Messerschmitt Bf 109s, but the bulk of the Luftwaffe 'Armada' were made up of Hispano Aviación HA-1112 M1L – a version of the Bf 109 manufactured under licence in Spain in the 1940s and 50s. Nicknamed the 'Buchon' ('greedy one') the Spanish planes were also modified to make them look like original Messerschmitts and had their livery painted with Luftwaffe insignias and markings. One of the 'Buchons' used in *The Battle of Britain* movie is still flying today and was used in the 2017 film *Dunkirk*.

made the film extremely expensive in terms of budget, with the film costing an estimated $14 million dollars ($100 million dollars today). The ensemble cast included some of the biggest stars of stage and screen including Lawrence Olivier (Sir Hugh Dowding), Trevor Howard (Air Vice Marshall Keith Park) and Michael Caine (Squadron Leader Canfield).

TOP GUNS AND FLYING ACES:
Adolph 'Sailor' Malan

Born in Wellington in the Western Cape area of South Africa, Adolph 'Sailor' Malan initially began his career as a seaman, working first for The Union Castle shipping line before joining the Royal Navy Reserves as a junior Lieutenant. In 1935, Malan volunteered to join the RAF and trained as a pilot, rapidly rising through the ranks to the position of Flight Lieutenant with No. 74 Squadron at the outbreak of World War II.

Malan distinguished himself in The Battle of France during the evacuation of Dunkirk on 28 May 1940. Malan was awarded the Distinguished Flying Cross (DFC) having achieved five 'kills' and gaining 'Ace' status in the process. On the 20 June, Malan took off on a solo night sortie and shot down two Heinkel He 111 bombers, a feat for which he was awarded the first bar on his DFC.

By August 1940, Malan had been promoted to Squadron Leader of No. 74 Squadron. On 11 August, Malan's squadron was scrambled at 7 am to intercept a raid over the Kent coast. A day of fierce aerial battles ensued with wave after wave of raids following the initial onslaught with No. 74 taking to the air on four occasions. By the end of the day Malan and his 'Tigers' (the squadron nickname) had shot down 24 German aircraft with a further 14 badly damaged. The day has been enshrined in RAF folklore as 'Sailors August 11'.

As Squadron Leader, Malan developed a routine of 'leading from the front' by volunteering himself to fly the first sortie of the day before returning to base to carry out his administrative duties. Malan was a strict disciplinarian, demanding high

EXTRAORDINARY FACT

'Sailor' Malan had a unique, if unconventional, combat technique (see Ten of My Rules For Air Fighting) but was renowned for his fearlessness in battle. During The Battle of Britain, Malan and the other senior pilots of No. 74 Squadron abandoned the standard 'Vic' formation outlined in the RAF's Manual of Air Combat Tactics and experimented with different formations. One formation Malan favoured was the 'Four Finger' or schwarm formation first pioneered by Luftwaffe Ace Werner Mölders during the Spanish Civil War (see page 80). By ironic coincidence, on 28 July, the two great aces met head-to-head in a dogfight over Dover. Although Malan's Spitfires were outnumbered by 4-1, No. 74 Squadron managed to shoot down four Luftwaffe fighters and badly damage three more. Mölders' plane was one of the damaged Bf 109s that limped back to base in Northern France. Mölders himself was injured during the exchanges and removed from active service to recuperate.

Four Finger Formation

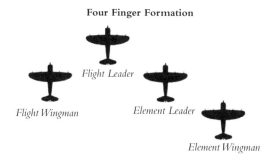

Flight Leader

Flight Wingman

Element Leader

Element Wingman

DID YOU KNOW?

No. 74 Squadron was called into action just a few days in to the war. On 6 September 1939, 'A' Flight was scrambled to intercept a suspected enemy appearing on the radar tracking. However, the planes in the air were actually Hurricanes from No. 56 Squadron conducting routine training exercises. 'Sailor Malan' and his two pilots, Paddy Byrne and John Freeborn, believing the planes to be enemy aircraft, attacked the Hurricanes and shot two down killing Flying Officer Montague Hulton-Harrop, who in the process became the first RAF casualty of the war, albeit as a victim of 'Friendly Fire'.

At the ensuing court-martial, Malan repudiated claims he had given the order to attack and testified for the prosecution against his fellow pilots asserting that John Freeborn had been reckless and impulsive and had ignored key radio communications. Sir Patrick Hastings, Freeborn's defence barrister, is alleged to have called Malan 'a bare-faced liar'. The court-martial concluded that none of the pilots were directly to blame and that what was to become known as 'The Battle of Barking Creek' was an unfortunate accident.

and exacting standards from the pilots under his command. He was also not one for handing out awards that he felt had not been fully earned and instituted a system for the receipt of decorations: six kills confirmed for a Distinguished

Flying Cross, twelve for a bar to the DFC; eighteen for a Distinguished Service Order.

No. 74 Squadron insignia

'Sailor' Malan continued in command of No. 74 Squadron throughout The Battle of Britain and The Blitz, finally stepping down in August, when he was rested from operations. He finished his active fighter career in 1941 with a tally of 27 aircraft shot down, 7 shared and many more damaged, at the time the RAF's leading ace, and one of the highest scoring pilots to have served wholly with Fighter Command during World War II. After the war Malan returned to his native South Africa where he made a living as a sheep farmer and briefly as a politician, campaigning against the Apartheid system that he fervently opposed. Adolph 'Sailor' Malan died in 1963, aged 53, from complications arising from Parkinson's Disease, a rare and little-known condition at that time. As a fighter–pilot Malan was highly aggressive and renowned as a dead–shot in the cockpit. An innovator and an outstanding tactician, Malan developed the methods and techniques he had refined during The Battle of Britain in 1940 and enshrined them in to ten 'rules'. Malan's 'rules' were shared across RAF Fighter Command and often put on display in Orderly Rooms at airfields to inspire and instruct younger pilots.

QUICK FACTS

• One of the defence barristers at the court martial of 'The Battle of Barking Creek' was London barrister and RAF Auxiliary pilot, Roger Bushell. Like Malan, Bushell had been born in South Africa and was captured during the war, later leading *The Great Escape* from Stalag Luft III.

TEN OF MY RULES FOR AIR FIGHTING

- Wait until you see the whites of his eyes. Fire short bursts of one to two seconds only when your sights are definitely 'ON'.
- Whilst shooting think of nothing else, brace the whole of your body: have both hands on the stick: concentrate on your ring sight.
- Always keep a sharp lookout. 'Keep your finger out'.
- Height gives you the initiative.
- Always turn and face the attack.
- Make your decisions promptly. It is better to act quickly even though your tactics are not the best.
- Never fly straight and level for more than 30 seconds in the combat area.
- When diving to attack always leave a proportion of your formation above to act as a top guard.
- *INITIATIVE, AGGRESSION, AIR DISCIPLINE,* and *TEAMWORK* are words that MEAN something in Air Fighting.
- Go in quickly – Punch hard – Get out!

TOP GUNS AND FLYING ACES:
Douglas Bader

After the release in 1956 of the biographical film *Reach for the Sky*, Douglas Bader became a household name in Britain. The story tells of his battle to remain a pilot despite losing both legs in a flying accident in 1931; his successful career as a fighter pilot in World War II; his capture after bailing out over occupied France; and his subsequent internment in the notorious Colditz Castle after his many attempts at escape.

Group Captain Sir Douglas Robert Steuart Bader, CBE, DSO & Bar, DL, FRAeS (1910–1982) won a place at RAF Cranwell College in 1928 where the eighteen-year-old soon proved to be an outstanding pilot, albeit with a reputation for being headstrong and prone to challenging authority. His outstanding flying ability earned him a place in the aerobatic display team where he received the reputation of being a dare devil. Despite being warned not to perform low-flying manoeuvres under 2,000 feet, as two pilots had already died doing so, on 14 December 1931 Bader attempted some low flying stunts, reportedly in response to a challenge from one of his comrades, and crashed. He was rushed to hospital with serious injuries but a prominent surgeon managed to save his life, though he had to amputate both of his legs (one above the knee and one below).

After a long convalescence, Bader managed to resume a normal life with the aid of artificial legs, so much so that he could drive a modified car, dance, play golf and, eventually fly a plane again. However, much to his disappointment, after being proved fit for active service at a medical examination,

★ AMAZING FACT ★

While practising formation flying and air tactics during the spring of 1940, Bader crashed a Spitfire at 80 mph on the runway, sustaining a head injury. Despite this, he boarded another Spitfire and carried on his manoeuvres. However, it was only later that day when he was having trouble walking that he realized that both shins of his prosthetic legs had been badly damaged from being trapped under the rudder pedals during the crash. Therefore, if he had not lost his legs in 1931, he would definitely have lost them in this incident.

the RAF reversed their decision, as there were no regulations which covered his situation, and he was invalided out of the RAF in 1933.

Bader took an office job with a petroleum company but still regularly badgered the RAF to let him fly again and in October 1939 his persistence paid off. At the outbreak of World War II there was a lack of qualified pilots and the previously strict RAF regulations were being far more loosely interpreted; Bader was allowed to be reinstated and, after practising formation flying and air tactics he was soon posted to command 242 Squadron which consisted mainly of Canadians who had suffered high casualties during The Battle of France. His style of command quickly helped to improve the morale of the squadron and they were up to full strength in time for the onset of The Battle of Britain.

QUICK FACTS

• In June 1945, Douglas Bader was chosen to lead a victory flypast over London which comprised over three hundred aircraft and, on 15 September of that year, he was given the honour of also leading The Battle of Britain Day anniversary flypast in a Supermarine Spitfire.

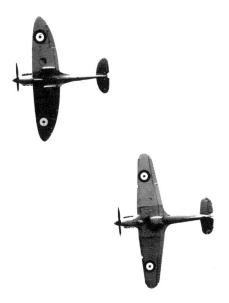

On 11 July, Bader scored his first victory with 242 Squadron which went on to play a prominent role in The Battle of Britain, their most successful day being 30 August when the squadron shot down twelve German aircraft, Bader himself claiming two. He was subsequently awarded the Distinguished Service Order (DSO) for his combat leadership.

Bader was an advocate of the 'Big Wing' tactic, which was supported by his friend, Air Vice Marshal Trafford Leigh-Mallory, whereby multiple squadrons would be assembled north of London ready to fight in large formations to give greater strength to oppose the Luftwaffe bombing raids. However, this caused much debate during the battle as the principal opponents to this approach, Air Vice Marshal Keith Park and Fighter Command Air Chief Marshal Sir Hugh Dowding, felt that its efficiency during a defensive aerial battle was questionable (see The Big Wing Controversy, page 99). Bader did, however, command one Big Wing formed during The Battle of Britain, the Duxford Wing, which consisted of up to five squadrons comprising Spitfires and Hurricanes and flown by an assortment of British, Canadian, Czech and Polish pilots. However, the Big Wing proved to be far more suited for the air sorties over Northern France during 1941.

Douglas Bader was awarded the Distinguished Flying Cross (DFC) for his services during The Battle of Britain and then, having been promoted to Acting Wing Commander, led his wing of Spitfires on bomber escort over north-western Europe during 1941. These operations were designed to entice German Luftwaffe fighter units into combat and tie them down from otherwise serving on the Russian front. Bader was renowned as a fearless leader, claiming numerous victories, for which he was awarded the Bar to his DSO on 2 July 1941.

Having flown sixty-two fighter sweeps over France between 24 March and 9 August 1941, Bader's Spitfire was involved in a mid-air collision with a Luftwaffe Bf 109 during an engagement and he was forced to bail out, leaving behind one prosthetic leg and badly damaging the other in the process. He was captured and hospitalized by the Germans, who treated Bader with great respect and, once he was fully recovered, Luftwaffe Ace, Adolf Galland, personally notified the British and arranged for replacement legs to be dropped. Before being transported to a prisoner of war camp, Bader was wined and dined by Galland as well as being invited to sit in the cockpit of his personal Me109. Subsequently, after the war, these two adversaries became life-long friends.

Bader remained a prisoner until the end of the war but during this time his characteristic sense of defiance and stubbornness did not diminish. He made numerous escape attempts from a number of camps, including Stalag Luft III B (which became the setting for the film *The Great Escape*), so many in fact that the Germans threatened to confiscate his legs. He was finally moved to Colditz Castle, which was thought to be escape-proof, in August 1942, where he continued to be as problematic as possible to his captors until the camp was liberated by the US army on 15 April 1945.

On his return, he was given the post of Commanding Officer of the Fighter Leader's School and promoted to Group Captain. However, Bader found himself spending most of his time instructing on ground attack tactics and eventually his enthusiasm for the RAF declined and he finally retired from the service on 21 July 1946.

He left the RAF with the rank of Group Captain and returned to work for his former employer Royal Dutch

Colditz Castle

Shell, where he went on to become managing director of a
subsidiary, Shell Aircraft. This role gave him the opportunity
to travel and fly a light aircraft, and he remained in post until
1969, when he left to join the Civil Aviation Authority Board.
He continued to fly until ill-health forced him to stop in 1979.

Bader was also a tireless campaigner for those with
disabilities and was knighted for his services to disabled people
in June 1976 and The Douglas Bader Foundation, which was
established after his death, continues to support amputees.

He became much in demand as an after-dinner speaker and
it was after one such event at the Guildhall in London on 5
September 1982, honouring Marshal of the RAF Sir Arthur
'Bomber' Harris, that Bader suffered a fatal heart attack whilst
being driven home, at the age of seventy-two.

BATTLE OF BRITAIN DAY:
15 SEPTEMBER 1940
'The Few's' Decisive Victory

Adolf Hitler

On 14 September Adolf Hitler
convened a conference of his
senior commanders at the Reich
Chancellery in Berlin. Although Hitler
had been pleased with the results of
the bombing raids on London, he
recognized that the Luftwaffe had not
acquired enough of an advantage to
proceed with the planned invasion
of Operation Sea Lion. Nevertheless,
German intelligence believed that the

RAF was on the brink of collapse and that the strategy of large-scale bombing raids on London should continue. In fact, the change in German strategy over the previous few weeks had given Fighter Command much needed respite, allowing time to rest pilots and repair air fields.

On the morning of 15 September, British Chain Home radar stations began detecting a large build-up of enemy planes heading across the channel. Keith Park anticipated that the raid would be in two waves and scrambled a larger than usual number of fighters in to the air. The Luftwaffe were taken by surprise at the number of British planes and the tactics employed by the RAF and many of the German bombers were forced to drop their bombs before reaching their targets, such was the ferocity of Fighter Command's defences.

The dog-fights raged on throughout the afternoon with 1,200 German planes engaged with 630 RAF Spitfires and Hurricanes. As night fell and the German planes retreated back across the channel it became apparent that the RAF had scored a notable victory. The Air Ministry released a statement to the press claiming that 183 enemy aircraft had been shot down with the loss of 29 Fighters. As was often the case this was considerable exaggeration as the actual number was 61 enemy aircraft destroyed with a further 20 aircraft severely damaged and the loss of 81 pilots (with a further 63 captured). However, the 15 September proved to be a turning point in The Battle of Britain. The Luftwaffe had lost twice as many planes as the RAF and their bombers had proved to be ineffectual with many missing their intended targets and being forced to drop their bombs indiscriminately. Two days later on 17 September, Hitler issued a directive that Operation Sea

EXTRAORDINARY FACT

Raymond Towers 'Ray' Holmes was a British Royal
Air Force fighter pilot during World War II who is
best known for his notable act of bravery, while taking
part in The Battle of Britain. On 15 September 1940,
Holmes saved Buckingham Palace from being hit
by German bombs. Holmes was pursuing a Dornier Do
17 which he had damaged but not shot down when he
ran out of ammunition. Sensing that the German plane
was heading towards the palace and Victoria railway
station, Holmes rammed the German plane which duly
crashed to the ground but the manoeuvre caused the
loss of his own aircraft. Holmes was able to bail out to
safety but was badly
injured, although
received much praise
in the press as the
pilot who saved
the palace. Holmes
became a King's
Messenger after the
war, and died at the
age of 90 in 2005.

Buckingham Palace

Lion was to be postponed indefinitely, finally cancelling the
plans in March 1941.

It was becoming apparent to Göring that the losses of
planes during daytime raids were not sustainable. Instead,
the Luftwaffe, with varying degrees of success, switched to

night time raids and the strategic bombardment of British industrial cities. The lack of RAF night defences in this stage of the war enabled the German bombers to inflict extensive damage without suffering the heavy losses of the daylight campaign. It is estimated that the Luftwaffe lost around 500 aircrews during the Blitz in comparison to The Battle of Britain, which saw around 2,800 killed, 340 wounded, 750 captured, and 1,800 aircraft destroyed and many hundreds more damaged.

The 15 September is celebrated every year as 'Battle of Britain Day', with events, memorials and fly pasts to mark the occasion of 'The Few's' decisive victory.

CONCLUSION

Although there is no official end date for The Battle of Britain (although many British historians often state 31 October) daytime raids by the Luftwaffe began to decline markedly from mid-September 1940. The Luftwaffe were also battling notable deteriorations in the weather conditions that limited the effectiveness of daytime raids due to poor visibility.

As stated in the introduction, there is some dispute as to the degree to which the RAF actually won The Battle of Britain. British historians draw a distinction between The Battle and The Blitz, whereas some German historians read that the Blitz merely represented a change in strategy. If there was a 'victory' it was in causing Hitler to postpone and ultimately abandon Operation Sea Lion. By the time daylight raids petered out the Luftwaffe were losing aircraft on an average daily ratio of 2:1. Britain had demonstrated that it had very effective air defences and, growing in confidence, was able to gradually go on the offensive. The sacrifices made in repelling the German attacks were considerable. From an estimated 3,000 RAF servicemen who took part in the battle only around half survived. Fighter Command lost 544 pilots, with bomber command and coastal command losing 718 and 280 servicemen respectively. 'The Few' may have prevailed to claim a morale boosting victory over the seemingly invincible 'many' of the Luftwaffe but at a staggering cost to human life on both sides.

THE LEGACY OF THE BATTLE OF BRITAIN
Places to visit – things to see and do

The legacy of The Battle of Britain and the memory of 'The Few' is enshrined in various museums, memorials and events around the south of England. Many of the sites described below are free to enter, contain interactive and immersive experiences and have visitor centres staffed by enthusiastic and knowledgeable volunteers and staff eager to answer questions and give guided tours.

The Battle of Britain Memorial – Capel-Le-Ferne

A permanent memorial to RAF pilots is appropriately situated atop the White Cliffs of Dover at Capel-Le Ferne. The site was chosen because it was an area known to the pilots as 'Hellfire Corner' on account of the many air battles that took place above the ports of Dover and Folkestone. The centre piece of the memorial is a large propeller shape carved into the chalk hillside with a statue of an RAF pilot seated on the propeller hub. The memorial is free to visit and has replica Spitfires and Hurricanes on permanent display and a memorial wall containing the names of over 3,000 pilots who took part in The Battle of Britain. In 2015 a visitor centre named The Wing was opened at the site which uses video technology to create an immersive experience of what it was like watching swathes of German aircraft approaching across the English Channel. The memorial was the brainchild of Battle of Britain pilot Geoffrey Page, who was a 20 year old Hurricane pilot with 56 Squadron and campaigned tirelessly for a permanent memorial for 'The Few'.

IMW Duxford

The branch of The Imperial War Museum at RAF Duxford is the largest aviation museum in Europe. RAF Duxford played a major role in The Battle of Britain and many of the original hangars which the pilots flew from now house the museum's exhibits and displays. Unsurprisingly the museum has a dedicated Battle of Britain permanent exhibition of aircraft, memorabilia and interactive experiences. IMW Duxford also has a functioning airfield which hosts several air shows throughout the year, including an annual Battle of Britain air show which takes place in the middle of September to coincide with Battle of Britain Day, where legendary aircrafts take to the sky once more.

Tangmere Military And Aviation Museum

Tucked away in rural West Sussex is the Tangmere Aviation Museum at the sight of the former RAF airfield that played a key role in The Battle of Britain. The museum consists of two large hangars containing various aircraft including replica Spitfires and Hurricanes. Tangmere also has a permanent Battle of Britain Hall with displays of memorabilia and artefacts illustrating the story of the conflict, including a section dedicated to Douglas Bader and a memorial to James Nicolson – the only Fighter Command pilot to be awarded the Victoria Cross during World War II.

The Battle of Britain Bunker – RAF Uxbridge

The underground Operations Room of No. 11 Group has been restored and meticulously recreated as it would have looked when Winston Churchill visited the bunker on the 15 September 1940. Visitors can descend the narrow steps down into the bunker to view the operations room where Air Chief Marshal Sir Keith Park plotted his fighter squadrons with maps and wooden blocks. Above ground, a state-of-the-art visitor centre describes the history of the bunker in a permanent exhibition that includes audio recordings of first-hand accounts of the people who worked there during World War II and The Cold War.

INDEX

Amazing and Extraordinary
Facts: London at War
Stephen Halliday
ISBN: 978-1-910821-08-4

Amazing and Extraordinary
Facts: Great Britain
Stephen Halliday
ISBN: 978-1-910821-20-6

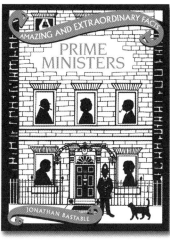

Amazing and Extraordinary
Facts: Prime Ministers
Jonathan Bastable
ISBN: 978-1-910821-22-0

Amazing and Extraordinary
Facts: Churchill
Joseph Piercy
ISBN: 978-1-910821-07-7

For more great books visit our website at **www.rydonpublishing.co.uk**

THE AUTHOR

Joseph Piercy is an author and journalist who has written non-fiction books on a variety of subjects ranging from history, popular culture and the English Language. Joseph is the author of *Amazing And Extraordinary Facts: Churchill* and *Amazing And Extraordinary Facts: Shakespeare* also published by Rydon Publishing. Joseph lives in Brighton with his wife, daughter and two grumpy cats.

AUTHOR ACKNOWLEDGEMENTS

The author would like to thank the following people for their help support and advice in compiling this book. Robert Ertle, Verity Graves-Morris and Prudence Rogers at Rydon publishing for suggesting the project and their help and support; Flight Commander Lenny 'The Hammer' Hamilton, Flight Lieutenant John 'Fingers' Forster and Air Chief Marshal Edward 'Butch' Dykes and R.L Lucas for their helpful knowledge, additional research, insight and sustenance; the staff at The University of Sussex Library for use of their excellent facilities; the staff and volunteers at RAF Tangmere Aviation Museum, my family and friends and lastly to my late Grandfather Frank Antonio Wiltshire, who flew with bomber command during World War II and whom I dedicate this book.

PICTURE CREDITS

P17, 50, 55, 62, 68, 79, 88, 89, 90, 95, 112, 126, 130 Bundesarchiv CC BY-SA 3.0; p38 Birmingham Museums Trust CC BY-SA 4.0; p42 Library of Congress; p110 City of Westminster Archive CC BY-SA 3.0; p113 New York Times Paris Beareau Collection.